200 TIPS for a SUCCESSFUL MARRIAGE

KENDALL DAVIS

Davis Publishing

Devotion and Vision Increase Security

Unless otherwise noted, all scripture quotations are taken from the World English Bible (WEB) 2020. All texts of the WEB are dedicated to the public domain. The World English Bible is an updated revision of the American Standard Version of 1901.

Scripture quotations marked KJV are taken from the King James Version. Public domain.

This book offers any songs, book mentions, quotes, or telephone numbers as a resource. They are not intended to endorse areas of the content of any individual's life and decisions regarding marriage and morality. The author does not vouch for the content of any sites for the life of this book.

Cover Inspiration: Dr. Makisha Davis
Interior Design: Bishop Kendall Davis

Also by Kendall Davis

Blessed on Purpose
A Daily Devotional on Christian Living

In His Image
A 365-Day Devotional Journey In His Image

Preface

I am a bi-vocational Christian pastor and admit that marriage was the hardest thing I have ever done. I always considered myself a kind-hearted, personable guy who could get along with anyone. Yet, to my dismay, I was married to the first person I could not get along with. I had two conflicting things inside me. I thought this was undoubtedly the woman for me. However, I would say, "This will never work." I wasn't alone; she felt the same way but spoke more about her feelings while I kept it all inside.

My first year of marriage was pretty bad. Some say the person you argue with most is the one you love the most, and I must say that I must have loved my wife a lot. Yet, as time went by, we started to deal more with our issues, both personal and relational. At one time, I thought the fighting would not stop, but now I can say that I have only had about four arguments with my wife in two decades. I have been happily married since 2004, but I have been married since 2000. I made mistakes after blunder after error. But I tried new things and learned. We can all get better in our relationships. We need a little bit of direction and effort. That is what this book is about. It will help supply the direction, but you must make the effort.

As I was working one day as a consultant, my job took me into a locked dementia unit. Inside, a couple was walking about holding hands. I thought the pair was cute, but they likely didn't know each other because of confusion. I knew that often dementia residents would mistake someone else for their spouse. She walked with a limp and muttered while the man remained silent and walked with her. After the third time circling the station, He said in a clear, strong voice, "Hello." I greeted him and later asked the staff if both were dementia residents. They told me she has dementia and walks until she tires herself out. The man was her husband. He came to the facility twice daily to help feed her and just walked with her for hours.

At that moment, I was amazed and flabbergasted. I asked myself if my wife could do nothing for me and didn't even remember me, would I be the man that would walk with her and hold her hand? I wasn't sure if I was that type of husband, but that was the type of man I wanted to be. That gentleman taught me more about loving your spouse than all the seminars I attended. That search to be a better spouse led to this book. I tried a lot of things. Some worked better than others. I kept trying and started becoming the husband I used to wonder about. This book will help husbands and wives be more thoughtful, considerate, and understanding. Let's work to have the best marriage because, like her, you may need someone to hold your hand one day.

Introduction

200 Tips for a Successful Marriage is a book of IDEAS (Ideals Dating Encouragements Acronyms Scriptures) that are fun, thoughtful, and uplifting. The idea is to cover every topic within a marriage. Think of it as a crash course on marriage. The tips are short and stand-alone for those who rarely read but varied enough to give the avid reader new ideas. Each tip is a topic about marriage designed to rest in our minds and make us consider safeguarding our marriage and promoting satisfaction in both spouses. Anyone who is married or considering marriage life will benefit. I encourage you to use it for yourself and gift a copy to couples you want to see succeed. Use it as an idea guide for workshops, small groups, seminars, premarital counseling, or to help someone struggling in their marriage. Two hundred tips give you a lot of material you can build on with your thoughts and study.

I am unapologetically a believer in God, but I endeavor to write something helpful to all who are married or considering getting married. Writing this book makes me think of the book of Esther, which centered around several parties, dancing, beauty, proper conduct, and a marriage that protected others. Esther was the story of the troubles of the Israelites who did not return after being set free from the Babylonian captivity. It never mentions God, but we see His hand throughout. We are each still learning how to live and best handle our relationships. Making mistakes is part of our path; learning from them and receiving wisdom from others removes the rocks from the road. I hope this book becomes a treasured gift that helps you along the way.

This book is dedicated to my wife and children,
one of whom has passed away. I love you always
and your support means the world to me.

Topics

I wanted this book to not only be instructive but fun. So, you will notice that the titles on each tip are not the tip's topic but song titles. These are songs you can dial up and enjoy. Each song is related to the tip subject in its title or content. 200 Tips is a book of STASH (Song, Tips, Acronyms, Scriptures & Hope). There are many acronyms if you love to teach, learn, or have fun. I have endeavored to use appropriate songs for all, but spoiler alert: they are not primarily Christian titles. You can't copyright titles; many songs and movies have the same name. See if you can figure out the song and who sings it before looking at the answers in the back of the book. If you are inclined, take some time to listen to the song to have a little fun and reinforce the topic's subject.

Back To God

Buy a devotional and read your spouse a scripture of the day each morning and pray with them. It will give you a good mixture of verses; they don't have to know how you found them. Most devotionals focus on positive and affirming scriptures and have a small prayer to guide you. I wrote devotional books "Blessed on Purpose" and "In His Image," partly to help individuals and families with this. ***DEVOTE (Dedication Encouraging Values Overcome Through Effort)*** yourself to the process. Studies have shown that couples who regularly have a devotional life reduce marriage conflict and divorce. If your spouse has questions about the meaning of the verse, the devotional will help you answer them.

Sometimes, arguments arise from discussing the doctrine of God's word. However, there are no disagreements regarding the behavior of the word. When we use our devotional time to discuss the ***TYPE (Template You Personify Eagerly)*** of heart we are to have and how we treat others, there is 100% agreement within all churches, families, and homes. Arguments arise when we stop focusing on our character and focus on the how-to's about things like baptism, communion, and all the myriads of doctrinal disputes. Keep focusing on what type of person each of you is to be, and you will find peace, growth, and fulfillment in devotional times.

Ephesians 5:26 That he might sanctify her, having cleansed her by the washing of water with the word,

All I Can Do Is Write About It

Your spouse must know you will never let go, no matter what happens. However, it's hard to trust someone who will forget the small but important things about you. What you know about your spouse isn't the same as what you will remember when it is crucial. Forgetting details is like taking them for granted. If you are prone to forget the little things, write a book about what they like. Buy a journal and make a spouse guide. A **GUIDE (Gains Useful Information Directory Experience)** can help snap the facts back into your memory. Make chapters one deal with their likes and dislikes. In chapter two, fill in the desires that they have mentioned. 3. Promises made by them and to them, 4. Things you do that excite them, 5. Their bucket list, 6. Issues with the past they need to resolve.

Add chapters as needed and write when anything important is happening. You can throw in plans, prayer concerns, or other things. Your **GUIDE (General User Information Directs Entry)** will give you the correct knowledge and a direction in which to go. Read it quarterly. Your spouse will be happy how you remember all the **DETAILS (Design Elements Telling An Intricate Lesson Specifically)** about them you usually forget. It helps avoid making mistakes and keeps us from guessing what to do for dates, birthdays, holidays, and other special events.

1 Peter 3:7 You husbands, in the same way, live with your wives according to knowledge, giving honor to the woman as to the weaker vessel, as also being joint heirs of the grace of life, that your prayers may not be hindered.

Love's Holiday

Our word holiday is a branch from the root of a holy day, meaning it's a day you set apart to celebrate. So, toss some confetti and celebrate your spouse's **HOLIDAY (Honoring Observance Legitimizing Importance During A Year)**. Start by creating annual marriage holidays. I like "Have It Your Way Day." What do you do? Well, the day is all about you. Check attitudes at the door. Pamper me and stroke my ego. You make preparations for this day just like any holiday. We have certain types of food for Christmas, Easter, and New Year's, so you should have your own menu for your holiday. Pick what you like. Most holidays celebrate a person's accomplishment or an event.

Your holiday is a day to celebrate you, so write out your story of things you have overcome and announce where you are heading. Make it spectacular. Read it, rehearse it, and revise it as needed. It could be private with your spouse alone, or maybe you want your whole family there. Make it your **OWN (Our Winning Nature)**. You may even start a trend among your married friends. Three months after your anniversary is your Husband's Day. Then, three months later Wife's Day. Treat her like a **QUEEN (Quality Unmatched Ensures Elegant Nobility)**. You can also have a Kid's Day in another three months if desired. That's every quarter, so make it memorable.

Deuteronomy 24:5 When a man takes a new wife, he shall not go out in the army, neither shall he be assigned any business. He shall be free at home one year, and shall cheer his wife whom he has taken.

Forget Me Nots

In an old folk legend, God asked a blue flower its name. It shyly responds, "I don't know," Therefore, the flower was named Forget-Me-Not. The thought and romance from the courting period often get lost in the marriage. So, continually romance your spouse by making a "Forget Me Not Calendar." Fill in at least one to two days a week that you will do something special. I had great success taking a calendar and marking days to give trinkets to my spouse. My **CALENDAR (Chart Arranged Listing Events Neatly Displaying A Recurrence)** includes flowers, poems, romantic letters, small gifts, picnic lunches, bubble baths, and back rubs. My wife began to leave notes on things she purchased that I needed, which made me feel appreciated.

Rotate the gifts so they don't get the same thing on a particular day each month. I would buy the cards, trinkets, and other small gifts and hide them in our home, bringing one out each week. It took me less than 30 minutes a **MONTH (Make Our Needed Time Happy)** shopping and never cost more than $60 a month to give my spouse a weekly **GIFT (Grace In Free Trade)**. I only had to shop again when I purchased fresh flowers. Husbands: it's important to send flowers to her job occasionally. She loves it when others take notice and show a little envy about how thoughtful you are. Wives: Show appreciation for everything he does. It will stroke his fire to do more.

Psalm 98:3 He has remembered his loving kindness and his faithfulness toward the house of Israel. All the ends of the earth have seen the salvation of our God.

Good Fight

To argue means to express an opposing view and give a reason to persuade another. To **ARGUE (A Reason Given Unlikely Expected)** is to disagree. Arguments occur so we can resolve problems, not fight over them. Your goal is not victory but progress. Never avoid conflict, but embrace it calmly. Arguments endure when we are too proud to apologize and stubborn to forgive. When you remove strong emotions from an argument, it turns into a discussion. When we are troubled, we don't have to react instinctively as a beast because God has given us the ability to calm ourselves and respond like people of honor. When feelings are strong and you don't feel heard, you may blurt out insults. Those are seeds planted that you will have to handle later.

You aren't the only one who will have to deal with the results of your actions, so slow down and think things through before you make a decision. Never make a life decision while angry, worried, or in **FEAR (False Evidence Appearing Real)**. Even if your spouse presses you to make an immediate decision, they can wait a few minutes for you to get it together. But this means you also have to give your spouse time and space when they need it. You can disagree and still support the person. You can learn to **AGREE (A Guarantee Regarding Enforcing Encouraged)** to disagree. It takes a little time and a bit of faith. Live beyond regrets and never let the situation take self-control from your hands.

Proverbs 15:1 A gentle answer turns away wrath,
but a harsh word stirs up anger.

Thank You

One of the most frustrating things in relationships is feeling unappreciated. To appreciate something means to give it value. Many expect their spouse to do certain things like give gifts, romance them, cook a good meal, or clean the home. Expectations are necessary for personal happiness. Appreciation is vital for mutual joy. Voltaire said that appreciation is what makes what is excellent in **OTHERS (One Taking Honest Estimate Regarding Someone)** belong to us as well. What you appreciate in your heart may bring you into what's happening, but your spouse may feel rejected if you don't express it. One of our greatest emotional needs is appreciation. Appreciation makes our sacrifices for our spouse make sense. It motivates us to keep doing what is good, even when inconvenient.

When we trade our expectations for appreciation, we find joy. It's not what you accumulate, but what you **APPRECIATE (A Particular Persuasion Requiring Enough Caring I Acknowledge Their Efforts)** that brings you joy. That's why you don't need much to be happy; you need the heart to be happy. If you desire nice things done for you, you should show people what they are worth. Callous attitudes eventually lead to callous relationships. Appreciate people for who they are and what they do. The feeling of worth and accomplishment you give will cause them to desire to give back to you.

1 Thessalonians 5:18 In everything give thanks,
for this is the will of God in Christ Jesus toward you.

Some Beach

Studies show that only 50% to 60% of people take vacations. Lack of vacation is usually due to time or money constraints. Some seem so content to try to live life after retirement, never knowing if they will even live healthy long enough to enjoy it. The solution to this problem is the mini-vaycay. Use local and national holidays to **REPLENISH (Restore Energy Properly Lengthens Everyone's Natural Inspired Spiritual Health)**. The average person receives around five three-day weekends a year. You may want to celebrate some holidays with family, while others celebrate yourselves by taking a mini vacation. A well-planned vacation reduces stress and fatigue and reinvigorates and improves our mood. Use websites and free travel guides with deals to help with planning. Off-season vacations can save you money.

Vacation means to **VACATE (Visit Actively Clears A Tenant Environment)**, so however far you have to travel for your mind to leave your worries at home is a good spot. A vacation is a change of pace and makes you think about what you want. Remember, you are creating memories, so treat your vacations as a honeymoon for the two of you. The rule of thumb is you only have to go as far as you need to reach an unfamiliar or infrequently traveled territory. That should be an hour or two drive away from home for most of us. Your time is precious, so **WASTE (When All Scrapped Trash Expected)** wisely to refresh, restore, and reinvigorate. Enjoy your vacations and live in the here and now.

Ephesians 5:16 redeeming the time, because the days are evil.

Photograph

When things go wrong, we often forget the joy we have had together. Create memories of the good times by taking pictures of several enjoyable events between you and your spouse and making them into a **PHOTO (Picture Holding Our Thoughts Optimum)** album. There are significant benefits to revisiting happy memories. When we intentionally recall positive thoughts, they decrease anxiety and disrupt negative thought patterns. Work together to choose what pictures to add and how to write the story. Add new entries every month or every three months and discuss the memories. You can add the day to your Forget Me Not calendar. Your calendar helps reinforce your relationship's **POSITIVE (Persistent Optimistic Support Imparting Truly Inspiring Vibrant Energy)** attributes and prevents you from getting too critical of each other.

If you're already doing this, upgrade your photo album by making it into a photo **JOURNAL (Journey Of Unique Records Noting A Legacy)**. Photo journaling combines journaling with photos by using written entries with pictures to record important moments, thoughts, and experiences. The photos provide for the visual experience, while journalling gives context to what occurred. Consider headings such as "Day in the life of" or "That time when…" Have a travel section, family portraits, meals made together, goals, and notes to yourselves. If you're tech-savvy, go digital, making it into a marriage blog that your family can enjoy for generations.

Proverbs 5:18 Let your spring be blessed. Rejoice in the wife of your youth.

I Swear

Wedding vows are marriage commitments. Our **VOWS (Values Of Wisdom Spoken)** contain the depth and meaning of our intentions and commitment proclaimed and agreed upon during your wedding. It's hard to keep a commitment you don't remember. Perform yearly marriage evaluations. Weeks before your anniversary, pull out that wedding tape and listen to your vows. Transcribe them and place your vow sheet in your marriage photo journal or anywhere you won't lose it. If you are about to marry, ask for a copy of the vows before the ceremony or write your own. These are the promises you made to your spouse. Write them down, evaluate yourself, and give yourself a score to see if you are fulfilling them. Recommit yourself to work on any area you may have been lagging.

If you do not have a copy of your vows, a vow renewal ceremony can help. You are creating new **VOWS (Voice Of Welcome Support)** now that you have a better understanding of marriage, and it gives children who were not born yet an opportunity to connect to what brought you together. Have an honest conversation about how you are doing with keeping your vows, and let them know how they are doing. Your **EVALUATION (Earned Value Assigned Legitimizes Using A Test Instead Of Nothing)** will strengthen your commitment to live by them.

Numbers 30:2 *When a man vows a vow to Yahweh, or swears an oath to bind his soul with a bond, he shall not break his word. He shall do according to all that proceeds out of his mouth.*

Lead Me, Guide Me

Counseling is a legal term used by those trained, tested, and credentialed in the area of expertise. My wife has a doctorate in psychology, which, as you notice, is reflected in the things I say and my writings. A marriage family therapist or psychologist may provide counsel, but Pastors and other religious leaders should not call what they do counseling for legal reasons. However, they can give spiritual guidance. People run to the **PASTOR** *(Person Applying Spiritual Teachings Of Redemption)* when they want to get married and avoid them when they want a divorce. The Pastor's role is to provide premarital guidance to help you prepare and determine if you are the right fit and have addressed the significant issues in a relationship. They also perform the wedding and help sustain your marriage through continued guidance.

I list scriptures in this book that contain principles that help increase our relational intelligence. Relational intelligence is a skill that helps build solid and lasting relationships, which our marriages need. Help from someone who can listen and direct you toward conflict resolution, healing inner turmoil, and affirming your commitment is wise. Don't wait until things get bad to seek help; do it to learn better relationship skills. Never be too proud to seek help or **ADVICE** *(A Directive Voiced Increases Cautioning Efforts)*. An ounce of prevention goes a long way.

Proverbs 11:14 Where there is no wise guidance, the nation falls, but in the multitude of counselors there is victory.

Mama Said
Knock You Out

In-laws are those who are related to you because of a marriage. That means they are family you chose to let in. **INLAWS (Inherited Neighbors Legalized At Wedding Services)**, only get in as far as you choose to let them. Relationships need a bit of space from outside the family. In an ideal world, in-laws and extended family should treat your spouse like they do you and never take sides. But we don't live in an ideal world. It's usually best not to confide your business to the family because they take sides. Long after you have forgiven your spouse, they still hold grudges. It becomes difficult for someone to support you in a relationship after they have seen the harm you have endured. It will come out in their attitudes regarding your marriage.

Before you invite your in-laws in, know how you will get them out. When your in-laws act as **OUTLAWS (Outsider Using Their Leverage Always Want Something)**, it creates an unsafe environment for your spouse. Never excuse their actions; deal with them. If your parents and family can't honor your spouse, they dishonor you. No one should feel comfortable saying anything negative about your spouse. If they do, then put them in check immediately. The husband's job is to correct his side of the **FAMILY (Father And Mother I Love You)**, and the wife's vocation is to correct her family. You're the new sheriff in town, so stand together and get things in order.

Genesis 2:24 Therefore, a man will leave his father and his mother, and will join with his wife, and they will be one flesh.

Get The Balance Right

BALANCE (Building A Life Addressing Necessities Creates Equilibrium) is not something you discover but create by setting boundaries and priorities. Boundaries are lines not to cross to prevent you from going overboard and instruct others on how to treat you. Boundaries limit your time on something, so you don't ignore what's important. Boundaries also keep other people's problems from becoming yours. Those disappointed by your boundaries are the ones who profit from you having none. Without *BOUNDARIES (Border Of Use Naturally Defends Area Restricting Invoked Emotional Stress)*, you won't have time to set priorities.

No one is too busy. It is all about boundaries and priorities. Use the *HAND (Having A Nice Day)* method. Like the thumb, God is nearest. He is first and strengthens you. The index points the way, and so does your spouse; they come second. The middle finger centers the hand, and our lives center around our children. They come third because you have a lot of life to live once they leave. Some seem married to their work, but like the ring finger, it comes fourth, which includes taking care of your home and working on your dreams. The little finger represents meaningful relationships such as church, extended family, and friends. Yes, church is not the same as a personal relationship with God, but you need others also. Balance teaches you what to keep and what to let go of. Never neglect the order, and you will find balance.

1 Corinthians 14:40 Let all things be done decently and in order.

Family Affair

Traditions are things that we value and want to **REPEAT (Replication Encouraging Performance Enlists Attractive Tendencies)**. They root us in the past and give us a sense of solidarity with all who keep them. The purpose of a tradition is to build community and unity. Your family will grow on the vine of your traditions, and if done correctly, they will become fond memories for your children. When families move to other countries, their traditions tend to follow them. However, we must treat our family as unique. Add your flavor to long-held family traditions and make them personal. These traditions will mark excitement in younger children and make older children gather together because it is their way of life.

TRADITION (Things Repeated Allow Dates Inherited To Influence Our Nations) is to build bonds, not to create bondage. You will be doing these for a long time, so evaluate traditions passed down from your parents. If they are beneficial, keep them. If not, throw them away. They may want you to keep their traditions when you visit, but if you can't, make sure you can explain why. The power of traditions is that they have meaning. The rule to traditions is you must be consistent in keeping them. Consider starting a few new traditions, make them your fun, and do things the right way. Examples: Game night (board games, cards. Karaoke), Family Prayers, Family Night Out, Picnics, Hikes, or whatever you enjoy together.

Mark 7:13 Making void the word of God by your tradition which you have handed down. You do many things like this.

Sanctuary

Your home is to be your sanctuary and haven. Home is where you should find peace and freedom from trouble. But you can tap your ruby slippers together and say, "There is no place like home," but if you haven't made your home into a haven, you will find yourself still at odds and in Oz. Like a ship tossed at sea, your spouse gets beaten up by the world. A *HAVEN (Harmony And Victory Emerge New)* is where you find safety in being who you are and scrutiny to know what to change. To make your home a haven, you must refrain from dumping concerns and problems on your spouse as soon as they come through the door. Concern is more crucial than complaint, so consider checking on them before you pour out more problems. We know you need to release, but give your spouse time to breathe.

Let them know there is no place safer than with you. Set the atmosphere by keeping the *HOME (House Offering Motivation Effectively)* clean and clutter-free. Make the bedroom a place of rest and conversation by removing the TV, social media, and work. Discuss problems over a meal or during a walk to reduce stress and friction. If you are weary, pray for strength and take *NAPS (Needed Action Providing Sleep)* on your lunch break at work. A servant attitude to help your spouse will relieve stress and give you the strength to serve, making your house peaceful and a place to be whole.

Psalm 4:8 In peace I will both lay myself down and sleep, for you alone, Yahweh, make me live in safety.

Roles Reversed

Never let anyone push you into a role that goes against your makeup. If you are better at something, don't avoid it because someone says it's not your role. It may seem weird, but I am a man that loves washing dishes. It gives me the same peace as gardening or some other chore does for others. There is no need to make dishwashing a primary duty of my wife because someone else thinks it's a woman's work. You set your **ROLE (Restrictions Of Living Environment)**, deciding what to take on and what to release. We work together to manage our household. There are particular things your spouse is better at than you. Your marriage is about how you can come together as one. The role you take should be the one you are better at. When each of us does what we are good at or even enjoy doing, the household runs more efficiently, and we don't get frustrated watching our spouse underperform.

We don't say a woman is not a woman because she works outside the home to help provide an income. I work, but if I also clean and do the laundry, I am still the man of the house. We are **EQUAL (Empowering Qualities Used Allow Liberty)** in value but distinct in makeup and do what's best for our family, not for someone else's opinion. Working together means progress, and progress leads to success. The decision and design for your marriage include your makeup. The best marriages use the best from both to make better things. So, the two of you are consistently winning.

Ephesians 2:10 For we are his workmanship, created in Christ Jesus for good works, which God prepared before that we would walk in them

The PayBack

Kindness must be reciprocal. Paying kindness forward has become a popular concept in society. Sometimes, you can't repay kindness, so you have to pay it forward by doing good to someone else. Being **KIND (Kindheartedness Inspires Nurturing Dedication)** shows you care. Some couples struggle because their spouse shows more kindness to others than they do to them. Good marriages repay kindness. Kindness improves our mood, so reciprocal kindness makes for a better marriage. The first step is to show appreciation for every act of kindness. Never take an attitude that your spouse is supposed to do nice things because it's their duty, and you deserve it. Deserving something means you have done something to earn it. If you don't show appreciation, you are already not showing kindness and likely don't deserve what they do, making your spouse feel exploited.

The second step is to **REPAY (Reimbursing Efforts Positively Affects You)** every act. Paying back kindness is just as important as paying it forward. Don't just be a receiver; be a giver. Never let your spouse outdo you. Suppose they do something for you, then do something back for them. Reciprocity will keep your relationship vibrant. Let go of things out of your **CONTROL (Command Of Natural Troubles Require Our Leading)** and do something about the things you can. You don't need to spend much money; be creative and keep them guessing.

2 Corinthians 6:13 Now in return—I speak as to my children—
you also open your hearts.

Listen To What The Man Said

Listening is essential, and listening to your spouse is one of the most loving things you can do. You must be attentive to **LISTEN (*Learning Ideas Spoken That Earn Notice*)**. For a judge to hear a case, they consider all the details and then weigh the facts to see if the case's merits go forward. It takes a lot of work to hear a case, and we shouldn't judge what our spouse says until we have listened to everything. Too often, we judge early and hear but don't listen. Your level of focus determines the difference between the two. Never belittle their thoughts. People speak what is in their hearts, so to reject what they say is to reject your spouse's heart. Paying attention tells your spouse that you are into them and love them.

Listening is a skill that makes us hear and process what is said rather than just responding to **JUSTIFY (*Just Understanding Supports Truth, I Face You*)** our actions. When you listen, hear their heart and what things they reveal are the most important. Listen empathetically by thinking **HOW (*Having Our Way*)** you would feel if you were in their shoes. We should also listen actively, being generous to give them the time to express their thoughts and provide feedback so they understand that you hear them. Your responses should show your spouse that you are with them, not against them, especially when the conversation deals with acts of other people that may affect your household.

Mark 4:24 He said to them, "Take heed what you hear.
With whatever measure you measure, it will be measured
to you; and more will be given to you who hear.

Responsibility

You didn't have a shotgun wedding where someone forced you to marry. Your marriage was not a mistake. It was a decision, so **OWN (Our Work Needed)** up to it. We should look before we leap, and we jumped the broom anyway. Though marriage is an obligation to live your life with someone, you should think of that obligation as a pleasure. We should consider obligations as responsibilities to do something good for our family and life. The more choices we make, the more the choices make us. It is your marriage, and you make of it what you wish. The goal is to take ownership to organize and move your family towards your dreams.

Responsibility is response-ability. It is our capacity to **ACCEPT (A Conscious Consent Easing Personal Temperaments)** and take ownership of what lies before us. That means we can change things if we control our responses. Commitment connects us to whatever we take responsibility for. How you act will impact your marriage and your life. We treat things more carefully when we own them. A responsible person knows the **ANSWER (A Noted Statement With Ernest Response)** to their problems is usually in them. Owning your relationship is about your integrity and maturity. It will help you to grow with each other rather than growing apart. The moment we take responsibility, we have the power to change our lives. If there is a problem, don't complain about it. You have the power to own it, remake it, and fix it.

Galatians 6:5 For each man will bear his own burden.

Growing Pains

Growing **PAINS (Problems Achieved In Negative Situations)** are not problems as much as opportunities. Some children feel pain in their bodies during growth spurts. Growth pains are natural and to be expected. You try to endure and seem to be getting nowhere, but growth is happening. In relationships, growing pains occur as two people adjust to each other. You have to deal with their habits and your pet peeves. Giving up bad habits is hard; dismissing your pet peeves is harder. The little things you fuss about don't always mean you are having problems. It means you are growing. Understanding growth will help you adjust when attitudes arise.

The first growing **PAIN (Perception Against Internal Negatives)** you have to adjust to is divorcing the mindset of a single person who could do anything they wanted and marrying the idea that you have to consider the wishes and desires of another person before making decisions. That's the hard part. Adjusting means giving up your whims to socialize with certain crowds, spend without thinking of goals and responsibilities, and **STEER (Successful Time Evaluating Evidence Required)** your ship. It requires taking two sets of perceptions and expectations and merging them into one set of goals and perspectives. Move and work together. Regardless of your feelings, steer your life in the right direction, and you will reach your goal.

Isaiah 53:2 For he grew up before him as a tender plant, and as a root out of dry ground. He has no good looks or majesty. When we see him, there is no beauty that we should desire him.

For The Love Of Money

Success isn't about what you have but what you can do with what you have. You will eventually go through tough times. To soften the blow, get ready now. Prepare for future events and attacks by savings. Remember those days of not wanting anything? Many of us think back to when we had money to blow. Well, you never had money to blow; you had money to save. Your goal is not to make money but to keep it. *SAVE (Securing A Valuable Early)* up because those times you had extra were to prepare you for a future drought. Put away what you can to be prepared for times of lack. When the unexpected comes, you will be glad that you're prepared. Saving will help you weather the storm without too much damage to your home.

Live as if all your money is assigned and only *SPEND (Something Paid Expending Needed Dollars)* what remains after you save. Assign your money to ensure you take care of all your needs before you waste it. Try living by the 20-80 plan. When you get paid, take 10% and give it to your church, charities, or some philanthropic means. Take another 10% and pay yourself by saving and investing. Once you have saved three months of emergency income, your monthly 10% goes into an income-earning investment account. Then, live off of the 80% that remains. It may seem challenging, but it is doable if you put in the effort. Couples who apply financial literacy and rules grow in wealth, and their primary income sources grow.

Proverbs 21:20 There is precious treasure and oil in the dwelling of the wise, but a foolish man swallows it up.

I Won't Back Down

Dividing and conquering is the most potent strategy to ensure defeat. It causes mistrust and confusion so that people will be at odds with one another. We are to fight with (alongside) our spouse rather than with (against) them. The worst thing you can do is let your inner turmoil and problems cause you to look at them otherwise. **PROTECT (Promoting Respect Organizing Tactics Effectively Calm Troubles)** each other. It is the two of you against the world, so have each other backs when people come after one. Resist them together, knowing how to fight.

Too many people are gunning for you to take **SHOTS (Spoken Hostility Or Targeting Someone)** at your spouse. They are not the enemy, so don't attack them. The enemy is the confusion that comes between you. When confusion comes, attack the situation, not the person. Settlers in the Old West would **CIRCLE (Create Intact Round Curving Looping Enclosure)** their wagons when attacked, and they used a strategy where they fought what was in front of them and depended on their partners to protect their backs. Their lives depended on each other, just as your marriage now depends on how you fight. As life partners, you fight back-to-back. Never let family, friends, or circumstances take your eyes off the enemy fighting you behind the scenes. Never let anyone divide you because after they have, then comes the conquering.

Nehemiah 4:14 *I looked, and rose up, and said to the nobles, to the rulers, and to the rest of the people, "Don't be afraid of them! Remember the Lord, who is great and awesome, and fight for your brothers, your sons, your daughters, your wives, and your houses."*

Faithful

Your marriage bed is more than a place for sex and sleep. It is a sacred space where you build on your marriage. Use your bed wisely. Couples should have a healthy sex life based on what they agree about and enjoy. The general rule is that anything unacceptable on your wedding night, such as adultery, threesomes, and swaps, leads to mistrust and harms the marriage over the long term. Remember, your spouse is not a sex toy. The male sex drive peaks *YOUNG (Youthful Optimism Unleashes New Growth)*, and the female sex drive *PEAKS (Pinnacle Erotic Arousal Kick Starts)* later. Have intercourse often enough to deal with your spouse's peaks without damaging or draining yourself.

The various terms used for sexual activity (lovemaking, intercourse, sex, procreation, consummation, and mating) describe its six purposes. Lovemaking is to express intimacy with your spouse and accompanies romance. Intercourse is a means of communicating your wants. *SEX (Sacred Energy Xchange)* refers to doing the act for each other's enjoyment. Procreation is for having children, and if you think of sex as only a means to procreate, you won't have much of it. We consummate our marriage to close the deal and sometimes use sex to get something else we want. Mating refers to bringing unity. Fulfilled sexual relationships within a marriage bring unity and intimacy in a couple to help them enjoy each other and communicate through marriage and raising children. So, keep it undefiled.

Hebrews 13:4 Let marriage be held in honor
among all, and let the bed be undefiled;
but God will judge the sexually immoral and adulterers.

Blame's On Me

Blaming others is like playing a giant game of "He said, she said." It goes back and forth, getting you nowhere. We all **MISTAKE (My Inaccurate Steps Taken Are Known Errors)** things, and rather than covering our mistakes and helping us through, some spouses point fingers at each other. Blame is easy but not productive. It has created many problems in marriage but has never solved one. The habit of blaming comes from denial and projection. Denial protects our thoughts and esteem and keeps us from mentally processing what we don't want to admit. Projection displaces thoughts and feelings. If you keep projecting, you won't solve anything. Instead of projecting, think of your spouse as a project that works on themselves as you work on yourself.

Take a serious look at your role in any dispute. Who is more at fault when you also did wrong doesn't matter. It takes two to tango, so take the lead and be responsible for your reactions. Try as you may, you can't fix your spouse. You can only fix yourself. When we resist playing the **BLAME (Being Liable And Making Excuses)** game, we empower ourselves to control and solve what is occurring. If you're working on yourself, you won't have time to worry about what your spouse does or doesn't do. So, stop the blame and keep moving **FORWARD (Forces Organized, Readying War And Rapidly Deploying)**.

Genesis 3:12 The man said, "The woman whom you gave to be with me, she gave me fruit from the tree, and I ate it."

I'll Be There

A superhero stands up for others when they cannot stand up for themselves. As a married couple, your rights are not limited to making medical and other decisions if they become physically incapacitated. The best way to **STAND (Support Taken Allows Needed Defense)** by your spouse is to stand up for them. They need a defender when they are not around or unable to stand for themselves. Perhaps they are being disrespected, disregarded, or alienated; you must challenge the one doing so and let them know you won't tolerate what they are saying or doing. Being a defender shows loyalty and goes a long way in building or rebuilding trust.

DEFENSE (Determination Entering Fight Encourages New Strength Emerges) is about setting a boundary others cannot cross, but that doesn't mean you should be foul. You can defend your spouse without being offensive. Though your spouse may agree with your heart for standing up, they may not agree with your actions if you become overly aggressive. Your spouse is not always right, but they are still the one you have chosen. Show unity in front of the children and talk behind closed doors. Sometimes, you may have to correct your spouse in private after you defend them in public. Do so in love with the goal of closing the **DOOR (Discovery Of Opportunity Received)** to future conflicts involving others. Just be a defender they can rely on.

Psalm 133:1 A Song of Ascents. By David. See how good and how pleasant it is for brothers to live together in unity!

Respect

Regardless of appearances, your husband's #1 need is not your body, neither is it your love. Above anything else, men want to be honored. Men generally love cars. *CARS* is an acronym for how men receive honor, which stands for *(Consideration, Admiration, Respect, & Support)*. Consideration deals with being upfront and including him rather than ignoring his thoughts. He also wants your admiration or for you to think well of him. Let him know that you are his biggest fan. However, his big ask is respect. Ask a man if he would prefer a woman who loved him but disrespected him or a woman who respected him but did not love him. He would overwhelmingly choose respect.

Men live for respect and die for respect. *RESPECT (Recognized Esteem Shows People Ernest Character Traits)* is the best gift you can give him. Rounding out the list is support. He also needs your support, just as you want him to support your endeavors. Sometimes honoring your husband is challenging, especially if you consider him part of your problems. Practice thinking of him as remarkable. Tell him he is honored if you want to jump-start your husband's heart. It is a salute to his heart and what it means for him to be a man. *HONOR (Having Officially Noticed Our Respect)* lifts a man's attitude; when they receive it, they tend to repeat behaviors that bring tremendous honor.

Proverbs 12:4 a worthy woman is the crown of her husband, but a disgraceful wife is as rottenness in his bones.

Don't Let Me Get Me

A woman's #1 need is security. If she is insecure about her mate, home, or position, you will have problems. It is difficult for a wife to follow her husband's lead when she has to provide for and protect herself. Insecurity leads to issues of mistrust. To her, security brings peace of mind and allows her to be comfortable to open up and trust you with her womanhood. Work hard to *SECURE (Safety Ensures Confidence Using Respectful Encouragement)* her spiritually, financially, and emotionally. Insecurity is why many husbands haven't seen the woman their wives could be. She only lets her femineity and vulnerability out when she is secure.

Security is more than just financial provision and protection. Those are just the *BASICS (Building A Strategy Is Considered Smart)*. There are many areas you must secure. You must secure her place by showing her no person is more important than her. You must be *HONEST (Healing Offense Needs Everyone Speaking Truth)* to secure your wife from mistrust and doubt. The husband secures his wife from his past by not comparing her to other women and having no contact with an ex. Make sure you talk about commitment and never mention divorce because she won't know if she can trust you not to leave her. Most importantly, communicate faithfulness. Don't look at others giving cause to suspect you of anything. Your wife is the prize, so keep your eyes on her.

Ephesians 5:25 Husbands, love your wives, even as Christ also loved the assembly and gave himself up for her.

In My Head

Your spouse should be at the top of your list but not the subject of the list. Your spouse is not a product to inventory, so eliminate the lists. Before you were married, it was the best time to discuss expectations. However, many of us maintain a mental **LIST (Log Imagining Spouse Transformation)** for our spouses to conform to. We give them silent but angry treatment when they don't meet our criteria. Lists create disappointments for us on things they never knew they were appointed to do. What would you say if someone made you a doctor's appointment and didn't inform you? The doctor's office would call you and say you missed your appointment, and you would respond in frustration that you never knew you had one. That is precisely what unspoken expectations do.

Most of us expect **MUCH (More Use Can Help)** from our spouse but only a little from ourselves. We list all we want our spouse to be without room for error. Let me ask you this. Would you fit if your spouse would make a list describing the person they wanted? If not, maybe you should reexamine your list for them. Lists are often changes you want made so you don't have to accept who your spouse is. If you need to keep a list, start by rewriting and clarifying it to just a few main things. **SIMPLIFY (Streamlining It Makes Problems Little In Facing You)** your list, and you will simplify your life.

Proverbs 18:22 Whoever finds a wife finds a good thing, and obtains favor of Yahweh.

It's Nice To Have A Friend

Marriage doesn't disqualify you from having friends. If anything, it should grow your friendship pool. When you were single, your **FRIEND (Family Recently Included Enriches Natural Dynamic)** was all your own, but now that you are one, you need mutual friends. Strong marriages have a robust support system. Friendships with like-minded couples help ensure that you receive encouragement and counsel through good and bad times. Having **FRIENDS (Forming Relationships In Enjoyable New Deal Supported)** with healthy marriages who will support your marriage and challenge you when making wrong decisions can strengthen your resolve to stay together through the worst times.

There are reasons we see record amounts of singles. Not everyone has a mind for marriage, and some of your single friends may not adjust well to your marriage. You are on a new team and will be running new plays. You can no longer be their wingman or wingwoman. You cannot spend the same time with them as you did previously. They shouldn't make the **CUT (Consider Use Terminated)** if they view your spouse as a spoiler. Having friends who don't like or have a problem with your spouse is like a bottle of nitroglycerine. Shake it a little, and you will have a big explosion. Married friends tend not to shake the ship and provide what other marriages need.

Proverbs 18:24 A man of many companions may be ruined, but there is a friend who sticks closer than a brother.

Hear Me

Disregarding advice happens a lot more frequently than most realize. We **HEAR (Having Ears Allows Response)** things that may sound like solid advice, but we don't act upon it for some reason. However, we should take special care to listen to advice from our spouses. Our spouses know or are learning to know us better than anyone else. As couples, we can be hard-headed, and often, our spouse has the answer to our dilemma. If you take your spouse's advice and things don't go as planned, your spouse is automatically part of the solution process. Fixing the problem becomes the focus because they helped get you into it. They won't be able to blame or belittle you for doing what they agreed to and recommended.

Even if your spouse's advice isn't the best, it should still be recognized. You don't want to create additional problems by belittling or ignoring them when they give advice. Just consider when you were well-intentioned but not well-informed, giving advice that didn't measure up. Heed what they said, whether it was driving directions or advice to stop doing something to get more sleep. Listening helps them to feel **HEARD (Having Ears Alert Reduces Damage)** and prevents jealousy in cases where you take advice from someone they are uncomfortable with. You will save yourself from a lot of problems down the road.

Genesis 21:12 God said to Abraham, "Don't let it be grievous in your sight because of the boy, and because of your servant. In all that Sarah says to you, listen to her voice. For your offspring will be named through Isaac.

Roar

If you have never seen a wedding lasso, it is a decorative **ROPE (Real Object Pulling Everyone)** laid on the couple's shoulders as a yoke or tied around one hand, binding them together. The purpose is to celebrate your unity. Other alternatives exist, such as unity candles/sand or jumping the broom together. Your marriage is a bond of two people; like any chain, you're only as strong as your weakest link. Your relationship has a Character of its own. It has been strengthened by struggles and cleansed by tears. The Character of your relationship endures because you endure. The best way to work on your relationship is to work on yourself. Men have greater physical strength, but emotional strength and character are more important in relationships.

Aim to become the strongest link on the **CHAIN (Community Helping Anyone In Need)** that keeps your family together. Rid yourself of those who corrupt your character and seek to align yourself with those who possess the character traits you desire to have. Be resilient and quickly share how you feel rather than holding in things your spouse needs to know. Flexibility is important. Sometimes, being the most forgiving can be the strongest; other times, it's being the firmest. **EXERCISE (Enthusiasm Xeroxed Employs Required Commitment Intensely Strengthening Energy)** is your total commitment and becomes the most vital link in the chain.

Ecclesiastes 4:12 If a man prevails against one
who is alone, two shall withstand him;
and a threefold cord is not quickly broken.

There Is None Like You

Most of our measurements came from practical things that were easy to compare. The inch was the width of a thumb; the foot was the average size of a grown man's foot, and the yard was the length of a man's belt. Easy comparisons are the basis of measurements. When we judge others, we often compare them to ourselves, thinking how far they need to go to get it together. However, we are not the standard against which to **MEASURE** *(My Estimation As Spouse Under Review Explained)*. When we judge our spouse, we often cherry-pick, mentally measuring them against our best qualities while ignoring the worst. Your spouse hates to feel judged by you and to be compared to anyone else, even you. Keep your judgment stick low and your encouragement meter high so you can make a difference in their life.

It becomes futile to **COMPARE** *(Contrast Of Multiple People As Rivals Examined)* how much farther I can jump when we both lose. We all fall short, so we reach as high as possible without bringing others down. Comparisons create competition, and judgment leads to condemnation. It is your job to build each other up. Whenever your spouse gets down, they look for the one who believes in them to pick them up. The lower the judgment stick is, the more you can help them escape conflict, criticism, and condemnation,

2 Corinthians 10:12 For we are not bold to number or compare ourselves with some of those who commend themselves. But they themselves, measuring themselves by themselves, and comparing themselves with themselves, are without understanding.

Ceasefire

The purpose of a ceasefire is to keep the fires from burning. Have a prearranged treaty between you and your spouse that allows you to shut down hostility. If things become overly aggressive, yell "Ceasefire" and immediately go to your **CORNER (Choice Of Resting Nerves Ends Rudeness)**. A ceasefire is needed when two sides are in opposition and are shooting missiles attacking each other. Our anger may depersonalize our spouse and hinder our ability to think and act kindly towards each other. The ceasefire provides a relaxed time to negotiate your feelings, preventing collateral damage from things you say or what children and others may overhear.

Your time in the corner is to cool down, not run away. Sometimes, you may need to **CEASE (Control Extreme Attitudes, Stopping Enmity)** to get space to calm down and breathe. However, leaving too often gives your spouse a sense that you will one day leave them. If you need to leave, go for a walk to burn off your anger rather than drive and make a dumb mistake. During corner time, only take advice from people who act as your cornerman and will tell you how to fight more cleanly and better. Then, you can return to the ring and realize that your spouse is not your opponent; your attitudes and circumstances that caused the conflict are what you're to fight against.

Ephesians 4:26-27 Be angry, and don't sin." Don't let the sun go down on your wrath, and don't give place to the devil.

Fast Car

Sometimes, we get so involved in routine courses of our days that we fall asleep at the wheel. Routines, a shift in priorities, and being too busy for each other can drift you apart. When you are not alert, you will drift away, feeling like you are growing apart rather than together. Drifting makes your marriage impersonal and robs you of the reasons why you are together in the first place. How far your mind strays from your spouse and onto other people and things measures where your heart has drifted. When our routines make your teammate feel like a roommate, **SHIFT (Swing Heightening Ideas For Transformation)** puts your relationship into high gear and takes it to another level.

Marriages are like cars. If you don't keep up with your regular maintenance, you will eventually break down before you reach your destination. Motivate yourself; you must **FILL (Faith In Living Lord)** up regularly to have the energy to drive. The wear and tear of life makes you check in to change the oil, taking time out together. An occasional marriage refresher seminar or retreat will tune you up and ensure your engine is firing nicely. The rest is just fixing a problem here and there, so everything is running right. Think of your marriage as a classic. No matter how broken down it gets, you can always restore it and make it more valuable.

Luke 9:62 But Jesus said to him, "No one, having put his hand to the plow and looking back, is fit for God's Kingdom."

All Of Me

We often tell our children to behave their best when taking them somewhere. Why? Because they are representative of us. A representative presents who you are in thought, action, and opinion. They have the power and authority to speak on behalf of another. Wherever you go, you **REPRESENT** *(Reflective Efforts Producing Respect Effectively Supporting Each Need Thoroughly)* yourself and your spouse. Your speech mirrors your heart, and your behavior shows how much you consider your actions will affect others. What you do will often ring in the ears of your spouse. Representing them means we mention them, stand up for them, and won't embarrass them. Just like we don't want our children to embarrass us, we should never bring embarrassment to our spouse.

When speaking in a prolonged conversation with the opposite sex, always look for a way to **MENTION** *(Move Everyone's Notice To Include Others Names)* your spouse. It makes people know there are boundaries they can't cross, especially if they are trying to test the waters. But do it naturally, such as quoting something your spouse says that is relevant to the conversation or saying what your spouse does positively. Remember, they are not a friend if they don't respect your spouse. The biggest plus is when you speak to your spouse later, and they hear how you mention them in your conversations, they will likely appreciate you for it. Represent your spouse in a way that makes them proud to be married to you.

Proverbs 31:12 She does him good, and not harm, all the days of her life.

Fresh Start

Sometimes, you need a fresh start in your marriage. It would help if you had some way of rebooting your system. A **REBOOT (Restart Efforts Based On Obstacles There)** returns something to the factory settings using hardware rather than software. It resets the computer's logic, ridding it of everything that has occurred since you took ownership of it. Rebooting allows the system to run more efficiently and recover from previous problems. When problems get out of hand, you may have to get away and reboot your marriage for a quick fix. A quick fix puts away the problems so you can concentrate solely on what brought the two of you together in the first place. It is about focusing on what you have so that you can attack your problems from a fresh perspective.

Remove the malware and start fresh. Whenever you **LOSE (Loss Of Spiritual Energy)** motivation for your relationship, return to the beginning. How did you meet your spouse, and what did you like about their personality? Perhaps they aren't the same because they lost their way. That means they have often given up something of themselves to operate in the relationship. The easiest way is to redo what you did when you first met. Go to your first date site and revisit some places you used to go, talking about how you felt on those dates. Bring up the good things and trigger the **MEMORIES (Most Experiences Mean Our Remembrances Incredibly Endure Struggles)** that revitalize the relationship.

2 Corinthians 5:17 Therefore if anyone is in Christ, he is a new creation. The old things have passed away. Behold, all things have become new.

Hey, Good Lookin'

Surprise them with a special meal with all their favorites. If you did tip number two, their favorites are in your journal. Buy it if you can't **COOK (Culinary Operator Of Kitchen)**. What matters is that it comes from you. Use your best dishes with your best accessories. Remember, presentation is everything. Make sure the plate, table, and environment are neat. Also, use a centerpiece for the table, flowers for wives, and candles for husbands. Play soft music to help set the mood for conversation, not just eating. Follow the meal with a relaxing evening.

Cooking together is a good practice. Not only does it provide quality time, but it also increases communication and cooperation. Perhaps one of you is better at cooking meats, and the other is better at side dishes. Plan the **MEAL (Mindful Eating And Living)** and set the environment by ensuring everything in the kitchen is clean and you have all the necessary ingredients. Work together cooking; the one with the least to do gets to wash the dishes as the other gets busy with other things. It is an excellent time to try a new **RECIPE (Rationed Efforts Cooking Ingredients Produces Eating)**. If they don't taste as well as you expected, the blame is on you both, so there is no accusation. However, if it turns out well, you have accomplished something new that you can repeat whenever possible.

Proverbs 31:14-15 She is like the merchant ships. She brings her bread from afar. She rises also while it is yet night, gives food to her household, and portions for her servant girls.

A Safe Place To Land

Don't **FIGHT *(Fire Internal Garbage Heaping Trouble)*** in front of the kids. Disagreements can happen anywhere over anything. But sometimes, we need a safe space to deal with them. Since arguments are differences in opinion, you can control them. However, fights are heated arguments that you have lost control over. They often include loud voices and hurtful words and end in long-lasting resentment. Children can be negatively affected, and if they witness continuous fighting, it can affect their feelings of responsibility, self-worth, and the development of negative emotions. You have two concerns. The first is to never fight in front of your children. The second is finding a way to do the first. Minor disputes may happen spontaneously.

You never want to let on what is occurring. Your children love you but take responsibility for things that are not their fault because of immaturity. Their emotional security is on the line. You don't want them blowing up at school the way they see you blowing up at home. If you need it, schedule a time for your fights. Treat fights as **SPY *(Surveilling People's Yearnings)*** warfare. Self-control is needed to keep things from evolving into a full-fledged fight. Use safe words to signal your partner when putting things on hold. Instead of closing the doors, you may have to sit in the car outside to resolve the issue. Take time when needed, but do everything to protect your children's safety, peace, and future.

Ecclesiastes 3:8 a time to love, and a time to hate;
a time for war, and a time for peace.

Body Language

Marcel Marceau is known as the greatest mime of all time. He expressed his story, displaying powerful feelings through the art of body language. Sometimes, your spouse may act like a **MIME (Mute Impressions, Mimicking Emotions)** and not express their feelings in words. Body language refers to body habits developed to display feelings without words. It is easy to hide your words, but our body language expresses our feelings and attitudes. Observe your spouse's body language. If you can tell what the mime portrays, you can learn what your spouse means by their body language and habits. Sometimes, our spouses are hurting, and we don't notice. Silent responses still communicate something. Sometimes, that stare may mean they want to give you the finger with their mind.

We also miss it when they desire our time. If we don't realize their **MOOD (Moment Of Others Distress)**, we can cause feelings of rejection or neglect. You should know that look they give when they want something of you. Take mental notes of your spouse's movements. Start by practicing identifying looks and gestures when they talk to you so you know what your spouse communicates when they don't talk. Not knowing their mood means you don't know how to speak to or approach your spouse in silent situations, which makes nothing better and everything worse. Heed their mood; you know how to help or enjoy your spouse.

Acts 13:16 Paul stood up, and gesturing with his hand said,
"Men of Israel, and you who fear God, listen.

The Dream Team Is In The House

Great team practice plays until they become second nature. They **WIN (What Is Needed)** because they understand how to work together seamlessly. Practice doing projects where you learn unity and each other's strengths. Some things the individual does because they are best at it. However, team efforts build cohesion. Start with team chores such as cooking, cleaning, and organizing. Try out a hobby that you both like and understand. Also, working together on a side business brings extra income into the house and shows you how to build trust and make things work out. The key is not just looking for something but trying something.

There are some things that you do together that work. The key is knowing your position and how to use it to make the right plays. Knowing the way your partner thinks is a plus. **TEAM** stands for **Together Everyone Accomplishes More,** and great teams win because they are unselfish and act like one. Think of yourselves as winning together. You are team _____ (insert last name). The more you speak about your upcoming victory, the more you will believe it. Unity in your marriage must become ingrained in your mind and heart. Keep the attitude that you and your spouse are the most incredible team ever put together. Work together, trusting & believing in your teammate/spouse.

Proverbs 27:17 Iron sharpens iron; so a man
sharpens his friend's countenance.

She Works Hard For The Money

They say a creditor is the only man who sticks closer to you in adversity than a friend. So, prove them wrong, stay close, and pick a budget plan that works for both of you. Couples in **DEBT *(Doing Everything But Trusting)*** worry because they spend their money before they earn it. When we buy things, we don't need, we sacrifice our future. Couples who max out their credit cards and can only make the minimum payments will quickly learn how much they need to budget. We must take charge of our finances before a lack of control leads to debt. When you wait to pay your bills, you often nickel and dime yourself into a problem. Small swipes on debit and credit cards add up, so pay all bills before you start spending frivolously.

Remember, we pay the price if we don't **BUDGET *(Borrowing Unleashes Debt, Giving Everyone Trouble)*.** There are many budget plans out there. Start by learning to pay your bills first, save a little, and live off the rest. A bills-first mindset gets you to limit spending and reduce debt. Once established, try a more straightforward plan such as the 10-10-80 plan, where 10% is giving, 10% is saving, and you live off the remaining 80%. It's about handling your business. It will keep worries down and help raise your credit score, getting you lower interest rates that will save you money because you are no longer a high risk.

Proverbs 22:7 The rich rule over the poor. The borrower is servant to the lender.

Work It Out

Sweat together to make you stick together. Exercise gives you *STRENGTH (Strong Training Removes Emotional Negatives, Giving True Health)*. Exercising together builds camaraderie and encourages friendship, understanding, and the discovery of strengths and limitations. The key is to consider each other when you do it. You will find friendly competition, fitness and a lot of laughs. Find an exercise you both like to do and do it together at least three times a week. It is also a time when you will find a lot of encouragement from each other. If you're new to exercising, start with stretching and low-impact activities. Water aerobics work great for those with pain or mobility problems since water creates natural resistance, supports the body's weight, and relieves muscle and joint stress.

Whatever you do, *ENSURE (Establishing Necessary Security Using Real Effort)* you like it so you don't quit. When you return home, you will communicate better because there will be less stress and friction from the exercise and the release of hormones, causing greater closeness. It's about togetherness, so even if one exercises more vigorously than the other, you should take the time to slow down and get your spouse going. It is something that spawns mutual encouragement and pushes you to mutual goals. Make an *EFFORT (Energy Focused For Overcoming Resist Trouble)*, and you will look, feel, behave, and live a better life.

Proverbs 24:5 A wise man has great power.
A knowledgeable man increases strength,

Ignore Me

Notice the little details and changes in your spouse's attire, actions, and attitude. Sometimes, they are going through something; at other times, they may seek attention to affirm that you still care and are sensitive to their needs. Ignorance is ignore-rance, meaning we don't know it because we have either refused, rejected, or responded wrongly to the signs and signals coming from our spouse. Ignoring something makes you ignorant of things that affect your life. **IGNORING (If Getting Notices Or Respected Is Needed Gradually)** leads to inaction, indifference, and ineffectiveness in relationships.

Everyone is ignorant about something, but that doesn't mean they shouldn't try to learn, especially when it comes to the person with whom you are to live the rest of your life. Important things are happening in the life of our spouse. We are ignorant of their heart and thoughts when we don't pay attention. Jim Rohn said, "Ignorance is not bliss; it is poverty." Ignorance is a curable sickness that takes a little time and attention. If you don't know your spouse's battles, it affects their thoughts, giving the **DEVIL (Doubt Entering Voicing Insipid Lies)** a foothold in their mind. You and your spouse are not to stand alone but to stand as one. Knowing is half the battle; the rest is restoring the marriage's truth, peace, and cooperation.

Proverbs 18:2 A fool has no delight in understanding,
but only in revealing his own opinion.

Role Model

Many couples have grown up with no living examples of what a loving, supportive, and successful marriage looks like. Those in troubled homes may grow up having couples on television as their only **MODEL (Mentors Opening Doors, Enriching Lives)** of what a relationship could look like. Some people have never heard of marriage mentors, but they do exist. Marriage mentors are experienced and mature couples who share their experiences and offer a listening ear to couples who are learning to navigate the landscape of their marriage. Marriage mentorship is different from counseling, which focuses on fixing specific issues. It is an educational strategy to gain a new perspective and focus on relationship building.

MENTORING (Modeling Effective Negotiation, Teaching, Or Relationship Intelligence Nurturing Growth) is preventative maintenance that enhances communication, strengthens intimacy, and provides support to help guide a couple through challenges. They can help both with growing as an individual and as a couple. A great mentor who believes in you can make all the difference you need. Mentors must be clear about roles, communicate well, and remain committed. If you have a heart for marriage and have experienced the ups and downs of relationships, perhaps you and your spouse can one day become marriage mentors yourselves.

Philippians 4:9 Do the things which you learned,
received, heard, and saw in me,
and the God of peace will be with you.

Baggage

Sometimes, what we think about doing and what we do doesn't add up. Why? Because bad habits, harmful desires & temptations interfere. Many of us have never dealt with our issues before marriage, so they carry over as *BAGGAGE (Bitter Attachments Gradually Growing And Generating Exasperation)*. Baggage is the emotional ghosts from past hurts that still live with you. Carrying baggage from past relationships will wear you down and hinder you from enjoying the future. The less baggage you carry, the easier it will be to adjust. Your spouse loves you enough to help you unpack your baggage, but you must let them in.

Everyone has baggage to *UNPACK (Unloading Negative Positions Always Creates Kindness)*. We must be honest about our motives, desires, and pain to heal in our marriage. Baggage means we haven't broken free of our past. Avoiding the problems keeps them going. It's about learning from past hurts and mistakes and letting go of the repeating thoughts that add weight to the soul. To unpack, we must remove the garment and realize they no longer fit who we are. Sometimes, this will take you through sadness, but it's okay to cry and grieve over the past so we don't keep living with its ghost. Having good friends around can help you unpack from the past hurts. Ultimately, you will feel lighter, more joyful, and more liberated.

Hebrews 12:1 Therefore let's also, seeing we are surrounded by so great a cloud of witnesses, lay aside every weight and the sin which so easily entangles us, and let's run with perseverance the race that is set before us,

Before He Cheats

When someone goes to court as a repeat offender, the judge makes the sentence more challenging to discourage the repeated behavior. People and spouses need to show corrective actions are in place to win your grace. Offend is spelled Off-End, signifying an offense is when someone has pushed you beyond the limits of what you expect and accept. Love should guide how you treat your spouse, but what you allow to happen teaches your limits. When someone is inconsiderate or self-absorbed, they will push to the limit and treat you how you have taught them that you will allow. Your **LIMIT (Level I'm Made Irritated Today)** may change with time, so your reactions or lack thereof will constantly teach them how far to go.

Givers must set limits because **TAKERS (Terrible Attitude Keeps Everyone Resisting Sponge)** never do. It's not that they make too many mistakes, but they make the same mistake repeatedly. Forgiveness is more about wiping the slate clean than returning to how things were without consequences. Always forgive your spouse, but if they aren't trying to get right, don't make it easy to come back in. But don't make it stringent; it's not punishment but teaching them your limits. You must have the courage to love and respect yourself even when you want to give in. When they know your limit, people tend not to cross the line. People appreciate what they work for. So, love them, but make them work at loving you.

*Proverbs 19:19 A hot-tempered man must pay the penalty,
for if you rescue him, you must do it again.*

Speak To My Heart

Catching someone falling is more strategic than digging them out of a hole. Whenever your spouse gets down, you must speak with the **CONFIDENCE (Conviction Of Natural Faith Is Deeply Embedded Naturally Coming Easy)** you have in their situation. Confidence is strength from within that prepares you to face everything out of your control. It means being okay with yourself if no one else accepts or likes you and makes you stand head and shoulders above the competition. You must show your spouse you believe in them if they don't believe in themselves. You become their biggest supporter and help push them towards their goals and success.

The critical thing about confidence is that we can **BUILD (Belief Utilizes Internal Leverage Diligently)** it within a person by showing support and treating their mistakes as learning experiences. We create confidence as they begin to believe in themselves. Even those with a confidence level of **ZERO (Zilch Effectively Remaining Obsolete)** can gain some. Your spouse may doubt their natural abilities, but you can see them. It is never too late for them to be what they always wanted, so never allow them to accept defeat easily but believe in the best. It would be best to redirect your spouse's thinking so they won't go into a funk, so encourage them always and comfort them when needed. Be confident in supporting them before they get too low.

2 Corinthians 3:5-6 not that we are sufficient of ourselves to account anything as from ourselves; but our sufficiency is from God, who also made us sufficient as servants of a new covenant, not of the letter but of the Spirit. For the letter kills, but the Spirit gives life

Playground

You are no longer a Toys R Us kid. Stop whining if you don't get your way. Temper tantrums are emotional outbursts characterized by negative behaviors in someone seeking pacification. Kids learn that these outbursts get them what they want, and some continue with this same immature outburst to communicate their needs. *IMMATURE (It Matters More Anytime Their Undisciplined Reasoning Enters)* adults throw marriages off balance. An immature adult is fun-loving and considerate when they are happy, but when they don't get their way, it feels like another kid is in the house.

Emotional intelligence (EI) deals with the ability to identify and manage your emotions while understanding the viewpoints and emotions of others. As we grow and navigate problems, we must learn to navigate our emotions in relationships. EI means dealing with our temper and triggers, discovering what sets us off and what sets us free. IQ doesn't define leadership, but emotional intelligence does. Sometimes, if you don't get what you want, it is a sign that you aren't giving your spouse what they want either. *IF (Independent Function)* you look to receive without giving, you will become frustrated. If you want fulfillment, seek to meet another's needs. It will bring unspeakable joy and maturity.

*1 Corinthians 13:11 When I was a child, I spoke as a child,
I felt as a child, I thought as a child. Now that I have
become a man, I have put away childish things.*

Rolling In The Deep

Two **WRONGS (Wicked Reactions Opposing Normally Good Standards)** never make a right, but they will get you left. Getting even may make you feel good briefly, but it only takes one moment to destroy your entire life. When tempted to get back at your spouse when you feel hurt, think again. You can't stop how you feel, but you can stop what you will do. Bad reactions only multiply an already confused situation. They do wrong, you do wrong, and then they do wrong again. Two wrongs become four wrongs, and four become eight, and so on. When does it stop?

CHEAP (Cost Has Everyone Appreciating Price) shots taken at your spouse are emotionally expensive. Sometimes, they are warning shots telling them to back up; however, they often come out so quickly and easily that they are misfires that do more damage than you want. Unfortunately, you can't stop the bullet once you fire a gun; you deal with the damage. It leaves your spouse as the walking wounded, with no one trusting you to bandage what you have caused. If you have a friend you confide in who tells you to get back at them, they are no friend of the marriage. **RESIST (Replace Essential Supplies In Sufficient Time)** the urge for revenge, do good, and let God work things out. Whatever ends up becoming of your marriage, you can proudly say you gave it your all.

John 8:7 But when they continued asking him, he looked up and said to them, "He who is without sin among you, let him throw the first stone at her."

Another Brick In The Wall

As we grow, we adjust to specific thinking patterns so that many reactions are automatic. People may tend to expect to know precisely how you will answer certain things, which can be good, but you want to ensure you aren't limiting yourself to old patterns without exploring new ones that may work better. Enroll in a class together on wisdom, logic, or philosophy. The goal is to open up new strategies for thinking and gaining wisdom. Wisdom has dual aspects. It teaches us the proper things to do to succeed. It also keeps us from making mistakes. Wisdom prevents problems just as much as it solves them. *WISDOM (When Insight Shifts Debate Opens Minds)* is not just the antidote. It is the vaccine to the issues of life. A healthy dose is needed to keep you on the path to contentment and control.

Discuss (Delivering Instructions So Concerns Used Should Stand) what you have gained and how to apply it to problems and *PROJECTS (Program Requiring Our Joint Efforts Can Take Support)*. Remember, the function of what you have learned is to think clearly with character. Acquire knowledge before you begin any project or life change. Preparation gives you the wisdom needed for immediate correction when issues arise. Knowing how to address problems together allows you to focus on the solution instead of wasting time on the problem. Couples who focus on problems often fail to see the solution.

*Proverbs 23:23 Buy the truth, and don't sell it. Get
wisdom, discipline, and understanding.*

Celebration

When we were children and brought home good grades and achievement rewards, we hoped for an expected emotional **REWARD (Receiving Elective Win Awarding Real Deeds)** or congratulations for our efforts. People tend to have a negative bias because our brains remember negatives more than positives. Positives build our self-esteem but require more effort to focus on and remember naturally. Never overlook the things that may be important to your spouse. No matter how small, each success builds confidence and gains momentum for future achievements and rewards. Sometimes, we assume that our mates know we support them; however, in their minds, you may seem like the only one who doesn't care or get excited about what's happening in their life.

Never let someone give your spouse attention in areas you don't recognize. You only make yourself look as if you don't care. After congratulating them, asking a simple question like, "How does it make you feel?" allows them to rehearse their feelings, reinforcing the positive emotions and building their **ESTEEM (Encouragement Springs Through Effective Empowered Motivation)**. Going further to celebrate with a trinket, meal, or special occasion makes your spouse want to repeat accomplishments, further building them up. Remember, their success now is your success in the future, so celebrate the win together.

Proverbs 3:26 for Yahweh will be your confidence,
and will keep your foot from being taken.

Notified

Spousal notification is the ideal way to communicate in situations someone watching may misconstrue. Business meals and meetings are innocent. However, whenever you speak to, chat online, ride with, or have lunch with someone of the opposite sex, you should let your spouse know. It may seem like reporting in, but it protects from confusion and mistrust. It would help if you were an open book to your spouse. If your spouse is uncomfortable with your relationship with someone, trust and listen to them. They are probably right. Mistrust fosters temptations to pry into the uniformed areas of your life. **NOTIFY (Notice Of Their Intention For You)** your spouse anytime you will be out with the opposite sex. You don't want someone to see you and tell your spouse something you did not alert them to yourself.

You have a spouse, not a work husband or wife. Adding other gender friendships after marriage to satisfy unmet needs is unhealthy. The benefits are not always sexual. Sometimes, it's attention, encouragement, and an unjudgmental ear someone is looking for. Starting a new opposite-sex relationship to satisfy **UNMET (Unsatisfied Needs Make Exchanges Tempting)** needs is unhealthy. Infidelity may not be the intention, but it can become the result. Notification not only protects you but also your spouse. It will stop anyone from coming to them and start confusion. Remember, all friends are mutual, and honesty is the best policy.

*2 Corinthians 8:21 Having regard for honorable things,
not only in the sight of the Lord, but also in the sight of men.*

We're All In The Same Gang

Problems are like bugs; never let them fester because you might find your house infested. The longer you wait to kill them, the more you have. Often, we address symptoms while avoiding the real issues. You avoid whatever you don't give attention to. Sometimes, we avoid issues because we think they will work themselves out. But they only work themselves into a knot and are much more challenging to handle later. It's good to **AVOID (Always Verify Options If Dangerous)** peril, but avoiding fixing something broken creates a more significant problem and a different type of pain. The longer you live with a problem, the less likely you are to put effort into solving it. It's like a low battery on a smoke detector that keeps beeping because no one replaces it. Some people avoid the sound and adjust to living with the beep.

A person avoiding problems is not seeking peace; they are just being a conflict avoider. **PEACE (People Expressing A Calm Equilibrium)** comes by resolving issues so there is nothing left to argue or attack. When we avoid issues, we compromise our true feelings and place problems in a holding space where they can return. Remember, anything we place on hold will soon become frustrating. We must stand firm and fumigate the home, eliminating those pesky problems. The only way a marriage gets better is if you make efforts to resolve issues and improve attentiveness. So, squash the bugs and reclaim your home.

Romans 14:19 So then, let's follow after things which make for peace, and things by which we may build one another up.

Were Gonna Have A Good Time

Turn your room into a private viewing theatre. Name your theatre, stream movies about marriage, and watch them together (without kids). They bring relationships into perspective and help us to think about what's important. Mix comedies with drama. Decorate your **THEATER (The Home Entertainment Auditorium That Exhibits Recordings)** according to your liking. If you work hard and are often tired, you may have to nap or try doing it early in the morning after exercise. Cry on each other's shoulder, laugh together, and discuss what you would do if you found yourself in their situation. It will help you understand how your partner thinks and learn from the mistakes of the cast. Pop some popcorn and bring the snacks. Make it a monthly date night for around $10 without leaving the house.

If you don't like theatre, make your space a home library and start a book club for you and your spouse. Explore new interests and discuss the characters after you exchange **BOOKS (Brochure Outlining Our Keenest Stories)**. It will clue you into what details your partner picks up on and what doesn't matter much to them. A home music, dance, or karaoke studio is another option. Certain things you thought may be a big deal may be unimportant to them, and small details may be the big thing. This information helps us understand how to relate to them. Enjoy your book club or private theatre, finding a fun way to learn about your spouse.

Ecclesiastes 9:7 Go your way—eat your bread with joy, and drink your wine with a merry heart; for God has already accepted your works.

Mind Your Own Business

If your spouse was a private person before you were married, they will continue to be so after the wedding. Keeping their personal life private from prying eyes is essential to some people's lives. A **PRIVATE (Person Requesting Information Violations Are Taken Earnestly)** individual limits people's access to things they hold as personal. Respecting that your spouse doesn't want specific details of your relationship to be made public knowledge shows sensitivity. Understand that there is a difference between privacy, which is good, and secrecy, which is harmful. Privacy is confidentiality based on preference and protection. Secrecy is based on deception and holds back information your spouse often has a right to know.

A second aspect of privacy is private time or giving your spouse **SPACE (Safe Place As Conflict Emerges)** to be alone with their thoughts. Remember, you can't see your reflection in boiling water. We occasionally need a few extra moments to clear our minds and see things correctly. When they say they need time, please give it to them. Private time is not a place to hide but a time to recuperate and strengthen and gather your thoughts. It creates a safe time and space to help a couple communicate more intimately because feelings on matters are processed. Be careful who you share your personal life with. Avoid friends and family that spread gossip like wildfire. Remember, your business is also your spouse's business. Consult only the most reliable friends when needed.

Proverbs 12:23 A prudent man keeps his knowledge,
but the hearts of fools proclaim foolishness.

Indescribable

From the Christian perspective, marriage is a covenant relationship between God and a couple. A covenant is different from a contract because contracts are between two people who don't trust each other. **GOD (Guard on Duty)** protects and provides guidance, and when pursued individually and corporately, He helps keep the couple together. Picture marriage as a triangle, with God at the top and husband and wife filling the bottom corners. God is our vertical relationship in a covenant, but the covenant of two separate people together makes it more of a diagonal run. Often, when the couple attempts to come together at the bottom, they bump heads and run into each other. But when each individual seeks to go up on the diagonal line, growing closer to God, the horizontal distance between them begins to shorten.

Growth with God equals **GROWTH (Gaining Requires Our Wisdom To Happen)** in marriage. As each seeks to get closer to God, they automatically come closer to each other. It's not just about attending church, which may help but doesn't save a marriage. Growth means applying the right relational skills, conduct, and respect to relationships. A step forward to leave selfish desires and bad habits while learning to communicate better is a step up in your relationship. Consequently, each step you take away from the Lord is also a step away from your spouse.

Malachi 2:14 Yet you say, 'Why?' Because Yahweh has been witness between you and the wife of your youth, against whom you have dealt treacherously, though she is your companion and the wife of your covenant.

Private Eyes

An Old English rhyme used as a mnemonic to prepare a bride for good fortune went, "Something old, something new, something borrowed, something blue a sixpence in a shoe." Generations of brides were lent items in a game by bridesmaids, showing the day's importance and heightening frivolity. Though **the RHYME (Rhythmic Harmony Yields Motivated Emotions)** is about what a bride is to have at her wedding, it is also an excellent concept for dating. The Ideal is to make a romantic mix of different dating excursions that change your dating plan into a dating system. The first part of your system is the rhythmic of having an old, familiar go-to spot you frequently call your own. It will carry your identity and memories.

The second part of the system calls for harmony as you try new things together. Some you may like, and others might not be worth returning to. However, the two of you are together, which makes it worthwhile. If your friend has an RV, boat, or timeshare, **BORROW (Bringing Other's Relinquished Resources Our Way)**, it sometimes. What they yielded adds to your day. The fourth part of the dating variety is something blue. Travel somewhere motivating where the event has a specific time, such as a sunset or sunrise together, including beaches, mountains, or scenic locations. The fifth and last portion is the penny in the shoe. Check your emotions to save a little here and there to pay for your dating system.

Song of Solomon 4:9 You have ravished my heart, my sister, my bride. You have ravished my heart with one of your eyes, with one chain of your neck.

Love Notes

Do you remember the days of the secret admirer? A secret admirer is someone with a romantic or platonic interest in you but doesn't want to reveal their identity, and no, they are not a stalker. Stalkers obsess over a person; admirers offer to let someone get to know their kind qualities before approaching them. It started with receiving a surprise love note, often letting us know we had someone's attention. From there, the admirer built upon the mystery, hoping that, like Cyrano de Bergerac, they would fall for their personality before even knowing who they were. Use love **NOTES (Needed Observations To Enter Summary)** to show your spouse you think about and admire them. Just like the secret admirer, you can anticipate what may come next.

The notes do not have to be very long. Sometimes, just an attractive sticky pad note will do. Often, your spouse will save the notes and read them to encourage themselves. Texting allows sending notes throughout the day, but unless you spend time to word them properly, they don't carry the emotion of classic **LOVE NOTES (Let Our Vows Encourage Nurturing Of Total Emotional Support)**. Leave love notes in places where your spouse can happen to find them. Use the note to explain why you love them because sometimes we don't know. Have fun and attach a stylish sticky note to purchases telling them how much you care. An occasional note with a flower on the pillow does nicely, and don't forget to give them breakfast in bed. Your spouse may collect your love notes to make a great memory, so make them great.

1 Corinthians 16:14 Let all that you do be done in love.

U Get On My Nerves

We all have our pet peeves. Our **PEEVES (Personal Exasperation Evoking Vexation Everytime Seen)** are little annoyances and are more about how we think rather than someone's wrong actions. We can react to certain sounds, smells, or actions we take out on others who are just being themselves. Being late repeatedly or not replacing the toilet paper roll when it runs out affects us slightly, but sometimes, we have strong emotional reactions. Peeves do not make very good pets. I had a couple who had issues with showers. Evening showers relax, are healthier for the skin and body, and allow you to get closer to bed because there are no smells or sweat. Morning showers allow you to shake off sleep inertia and get your day going. She wanted clean linens, and he just wanted to get up vigorously in the morning, an instant pet peeve.

Take a piece of paper and write the title "5 things my spouse does that **IRRITATE (I Rarely Relate If They Are Truly Exasperating) me**" on top. List the five things. Make them short and thoughtful. Please don't share them with anyone. Put the list down, then cross out the former title and write, "My prayer list." Then pray that God helps you and your spouse in these areas and that their actions will no longer bother you. When you hear about the problem, you often hear how to help. Sometimes, praying out loud is best because it helps you work out feelings like self-affirmations, helping the issues become less important.

Philippians 2:14 Do all things without complaining and arguing,

Got My Name Changed Back

There is a lot of training out there on how to protect yourself from an STD. Simply being faithful to your spouse will prevent it and its repercussions. But how many have protection from an LTD? An LTD is a long-term divorce. It occurs when one or both spouses have discontentment with the other for years and haven't dealt with it. They think about divorce for years but keep in the relationship for the sake of the kids or financial reasons. Rather than working on resolving their problems and feelings, they continue until they no longer see a purpose in staying married. Children see their families torn apart a few years after they grow up because the long-term **DIVORCE (Dissolving Intimate Vows One's Relationship Can End)** mentality only lasts until the need for stability no longer weighs on the parent's conscience.

Long-term divorces come from marriages that started right but lost their way. To **PREVENT (Practice Restraining Every Vice Ends New Troubles)** an STD, you have to change your mind and attitude. Decide in your heart that there is only one partner you want to be with, commit to making it work, and resolve your issues so no one can get between you. The same faithfulness to prevent an STD will prevent an LTD. You may be saying to yourself when the kids grow up or when I get more stable, I'm out. However, we have a chance to be honest and change things now. Renew your mind and get rid of your LTD.

Matthew 19:8 He said to them, "Moses, because of the hardness of your hearts, allowed you to divorce your wives, but from the beginning it has not been so.

When Doves Cry

Doves symbolize loyalty and love because their species are monogamous and are one of the few creatures who mate for life. They form bonds through their courtship display of movements and chirping, which equates to song and dance. They show affection by cuddling and will not even look at another dove because they dedicate themselves to one and one only. Too many of us act like pigeons and **FOUL (Fresh Odors Usually Last)** up the place wherever we go. Pigeons mate by a clapping display of puffing up their chest and flapping their wings to attract a female. The female pigeon shows interest by shyly cooing and bowing her head. The dove chooses its mate based on how well you treat them, and the pigeon chooses based on looks. We choose our spouse but act as if we don't know what we want.

There is fruitfulness in faithfulness. You should want to look attractive to your spouse, but how you treat each other gives you dove eyes. Your eye deals with your **FOCUS (Following One Course Until Success)**. When you reject your spouse's attention and affection, they may feel rejected as a person and lover. We also need to place our eyes on our faithfulness. Dove Eyes puts your spouse first but still has time to handle your business. They may even help you more because you respond to their attempts to cuddle or hold hands even when there is no sex involved. So, learn from the dove and keep your eyes focused.

Songs of Solomon 1:15 Behold, you are beautiful, my love.
Behold, you are beautiful. Your eyes are like doves.

Think

Professional speakers sometimes tape themselves to critique how to speak better. They listen for **FLAWS (Faults Lets A Weakness Stand)** in their speech to learn how to communicate better. Tape yourself and listen to how you speak to your spouse. It's not only what you say but how you say it. I'm not talking about taping and argument so you can find additional faults with your spouse. But tape your reactions to questions and conversations when you may not want to be bothered. You may find the attitude you project isn't what you intended. You may learn that you speak down to them instead of encouraging them. Use your tape to learn to speak better to each other. Tape yourself again to see if you have made gains.

Eugene Swartz said, "No sentence can be effective if it contains facts alone. It must also contain emotion, image, logic, and promise." There is power in taking a mental pause and thinking before we speak. Many words we say are rash and impulsive, so we put our foot in our mouth. **THINK (True, Helpful, Inspiring, Necessary, Kind)** is an acronym for filtering our thoughts through 5 criteria before saying something. We ask ourselves if what we are about to say is true, helpful to the situation, will inspire someone, if it needs saying at all, and if it is kind to say. These things will help our words build rather than tear our spouse down.

Ephesians 4:29 Let no corrupt speech proceed out of your mouth, but only what is good for building others up as the need may be, that it may give grace to those who hear

The Secret Garden

Sleeping naked isn't just for sex. It allows the body to cool down, allowing you to fall **ASLEEP (A Snooze Leaves Everyone Energetically Prepared)** faster and improve your sleep quality, which reduces stress and anxiety and helps to reduce weight gain. For women, it decreases the likelihood of yeast infections and increases reproductive chances in men. Adults also have a small amount of brown fat in their necks. Brown fat is the good fat found in babies that keep them warm. Sleeping naked may activate our brown fat, burning more calories. However, despite the health benefits, sleeping naked has benefits that make your marriage healthy.

Sleep **NAKED (No Attire Kept Exposing Defects)** sometimes just to cuddle. You need to enjoy each other's body without sex. Some wives fear cuddling because we men only do it when we want sex. Show your wife you can be close to her without only considering your physical needs. While you don't have to be naked to be sexy, sleeping skin-to-skin enhances intimacy by releasing oxytocin, which is the love hormone. Naked also means being your natural self and showing your spouse the real you. It's about being intentional and fixing your eyes on a greater reward. Sometimes, you probably will have to have sex the night before, so this can work. Try it, men. The more **CUDDLING (Caress Used Drawing Devotion Lets Individual Needs Grow)** you can do without sex, the more sex you end up having.

*Genesis 2:25 The man and his wife were both
naked, and they were not ashamed.*

Baby, What A Big Surprise

We have workplace boundaries in place most often to protect our marriage from outside interference but also to protect our job from a well-meaning spouse. Unless you work together, many spouses only see the inside of their spouse's workplace at the company picnic or the end-of-the-year holiday celebration. Work is where you have to trust your spouse to do what needs doing. Work is where your spouse needs to focus, complete tasks, and secure a better future for your family. It appears invasive for a spouse to visit their partner's workplace too often. Let your spouse finish their work and **VISIT (Viewers Intended Stay In Transit)** only when you have a good reason. But that doesn't include lunch and occasional break with your spouse.

Surprise your spouse at work for lunch. Cooking for them and having a picnic at the local park is ideal. If you don't have time to make lunch, get some takeout or visit one of their favorite lunch spots. Bring them a **CARD (Caring Aides Receiving Devotion)** or have a special dessert to celebrate them. Remember to get permission from your boss for an extended lunch first. It may cost you an extra hour of pay, but it will be well worth it. Not only do you mark your territory, but you also let everyone know you exist. You become a pleasant break for your spouse, and they will know you are thinking of them.

Ecclesiastes 3:22 I have seen that there is nothing better for a man than to enjoy his work, because that is his lot. For who can bring him to see what will come after him?

Brother, Can You Spare A Dime

Open a vacation savings account at a new bank at least a mile or two away from your home and destroy any debit card they may send you. A vacation *SAVINGS (Secure Assets Valuably Increasing Nest-egg Growth Strategy)* account is exclusively for travel, vacations, and holidays. They are beneficial in covering significant expenses when you need a getaway or have a lot of holiday gifts to purchase. This way, you won't have to max out your credit cards and spend the next six months trying to pay them down before you go on your next vacation. If you have electronic banking, resist linking it to other banks, so you must go into the bank to make deposits and withdrawals. The distance and inconvenience of the bank will help you resist drawing money out unless you really need it.

Remember that you probably live above your means if you never have anything to save. Save pennies everywhere. Some apps allow you to take the change out of your account and will automate savings for you. Know what you need and want to do. Reducing how much fast food, junk food, and café-bought coffee and tea you *BUY (Bargains Unleash Yearning)* can immediately save hundreds so that you can put some money away. It's about learning to save first and spend afterward. Consider putting money from bonuses or side hustles into your vacation account. It will ultimately reward you, so don't spend until you save a little.

Luke 14:28 For which of you, desiring to build a tower,
doesn't first sit down and count the cost,
to see if he has enough to complete it?

Sweet Thing

After a few years, we either neglect the pet name we gave our spouse, or it loses its effect. If your pet name has died, revitalize it. Use it again, or think of a new one. Remember, Pet Names should be related to something significant between you. Bring it out again and have fun. The **NAME (Normally Assigned Moniker Elicited)** you call your spouse affects their mood and thinking. Pet names come in the form of sweet names, romantic titles, and couple nicknames. Sweet names are flirty and speak to how you feel about each other. Calling your spouse honey or sweetie also softens the blows that a coming conversation may bring.

Romantic titles flatter your spouse and tell them what you think about them by calling them your love, handsome, beautiful, or wonderful. They build the esteem of your spouse and make them feel like they still have your attention. Having a **COUPLE'S (Calling Our Union Pleasing Left Everyone Stunned)** nicknames as your own, such as Bonnie to your Clyde or Adam to your Eve, have a complete story behind them that you can connect to. You can dress up as the selected couple and take pictures to hang in your bedroom or hallway. They help develop a mindset that you are in this together and have some of the same characteristics and meaning to each other that the couple did. Use your names to display your attention and attraction to your spouse and keep the fire burning.

Songs of Solomon 6:3 I am my beloved's, and my beloved is mine.
He browses among the lilies.

At Your Side

Do you remember being told that actions are louder than words? Well, it's true. Actions drive **RESULT (Reactions Encourage Solutions Used Long Term)** and create greater motivation. While words tell us how someone feels, actions display if that feeling is authentic. Before people started talking about your love language, it was plain to many that mutual service and sacrifice in a relationship are beneficial. Acts of service are activities that make your spouse's day or life a little bit easier and perhaps more enjoyable. I highly recommend that you read Gary Chapman's book, "The Five Love Languages," but an occasional act of service helps even when it is not one of your love languages. We need to focus on regularly being a help to our spouse so that they don't feel overwhelmed or drained of their energy.

Just because your spouse can do something doesn't mean they have to. Husbands, if you're blessed to be a two-car family, **WASH (Wipes Away Stains Habitually)** your wife's car and take and fill up the gas for her. If she has ever paid more at the mechanic, she would appreciate it if you could take the car for a tune-up or repairs. Wives get up and make him coffee or iron his clothing for him. Acts of service will not only help us improve our day but also our lives. When you see something, you can quickly help with, offer help, and be the action behind the **WORDS (Wisdom Organized Resolves Delayed Speech)**. A small action is usually all it takes to lift someone's day.

Galatians 6:2 Bear one another's burdens, and so fulfill the law of Christ.

1-800-273-8255

Having a spiritual home and relationship helps to bring peace and acceptance to our lives. God is called a counselor because the directions He gives us help us heal and have the insight to live life and handle relationships with a level of skill that leads to success. Sometimes, people of faith shy away from counseling because they have God as a great counselor. Yet, often, we struggle even to listen to Him. Having God doesn't mean you don't need a **COUNSELOR (Coordinating Our Understanding Negates Self Errors Limiting Our Reasoning)**. Finding a counselor or therapist consistent with your faith is not difficult. You may need that unjudgmental ear that is more concerned with helping you grow than they are being on your side.

A therapist listens like a good friend but guides the conversations in ways that help adjust our thinking and deal with our feelings. Having a counselor doesn't mean tuning out God. After every session, pray and use the **TOOLS (Taking Our Opportunities Left Standing)** you have learned. For every problem you can't handle, turn it over to God. He is the only one who can instantly turn a catastrophe into triumph. Some of us may have walked away from our faith or buried our faith in our problems. However, God is more significant than your circumstances and still heals every situation. Return to your first love and watch him solve your problems.

Isaiah 9:6 For a child is born to us. A son is given to us; and the government will be on his shoulders. His name will be called Wonderful Counselor, Mighty God, Everlasting Father, Prince of Peace.

Give Us Clean Hands

A big issue in religious couples is that one isn't as dedicated to their faith or is falling away. The **GAP (Growing Apart Persists)** in commitment is an area in which the spouse who is stronger in their faith doesn't feel support. If the spouse with the more robust faith gets weak, they believe the less committed spouse may not be strong enough to help them return to a meaningful spiritual journey. A man will come to Church even if it's just to keep the hungry bears away from his honey. If your spouse doesn't pray, some things can help, like attending church, meeting Christian friends, and serving in the community. You can't expect them to serve God if you don't.

But this makes our spouse the perfect prayer partner. Engaging them in habits of **PRAYER (Person Repents Asking Yahweh Extra Requests)** with you brings meaning into your relationship. When they see things answered, it will help their conviction to pray. Because of their love for you and desire to see your growth, they can touch and agree with you in areas most people don't know about. A prayer partner prays for you and journeys with you, going through the entire process until the issue is resolved. Revealing personal prayer requests helps your spouse know and understand your thoughts and emotional needs. Having them with you causes you to feel their care and support.

Luke 21:36 Therefore be watchful all the time, praying that you may be counted worthy to escape all these things that will happen, and to stand before the Son of Man."

When I Said I Do

The choice of a spouse is up to the individual, but there are places where arranged marriages are the norm. Arranged marriages tend to **LAST (*Love Always Stands Together*)** longer as it is a business deal that you work on. Due to social pressure and not wanting to disappoint the one arranging the marriage, divorce isn't much of an option. Having an arranged marriage isn't as bad as many think. Some start their marriage with so much love and hope they believe they are a match made in heaven. They have an arranged marriage where God supervises, selects, and secures their spouse. However, a match made in heaven must be shaped here on earth.

While in heaven, everything runs as planned; on earth, we must make adjustments. You have to be flexible when dealing with real people and situations. It's good to plan, but you must **ADJUST (*Adapt Daily Journey Until Soul Transforms*)** for unexpected things. The three most important things to adjust are our expectations, attitude, and independent habits. If we hold expectations built on personal desires, we exchange them for ones based on personal temperaments and abilities. Our attitude toward building ourselves is adjusted to build us as a couple, and all independent habits must give way to communication and concern. Adjust a little to make things work on earth as if they came from heaven.

Genesis 24:7 Yahweh, the God of heaven—who took me from my father's house, and from the land of my birth, who spoke to me, and who swore to me, saying, 'I will give this land to your offspring—he will send his angel before you, and you shall take a wife for my son fro-m there

Turn Off The Lights

We all have moments when we know it's time to come together intimately. Sometimes, we are making love, and other times, we are just having sex. Not every intimate time should be the same. Be **PREPARED (Plans Reached Early Promote A Ready Equipped Day)** for the romantic times when you slow everything down to enjoy intimacy with each other. It's nice to have most of the evening or a whole night privately without interruptions. Sometimes, the moment arises sporadically, and you must prepare to make it memorable. Make a love kit ready for use on special occasions or when the whim arises.

A love kit is a romantic toolbox you can use repeatedly. Think about having a silk blindfold, a teasing feather, and flavorful sprays that make you want to shower your spouse with kisses. Imitation flowers and petals are on the bed, candles are all around, you play romantic games, and incense and body oils are present. You buy them once but get multiple uses from them. You don't have to spend and spend to set the atmosphere, just a little music, time alone, and your love kit. The size of your kit is determined by how romantic you are, so shop wisely and save. Keep your love **KIT (Keep In Touch)** in a small bag or suitcase so you don't have to look for anything. As you think of new things, add to your kit. It will take only 10 minutes to set up, and you will have the rest of the night to enjoy

*Songs of Solomon 7:13 The mandrakes produce fragrance.
At our doors are all kinds of precious fruits, new and
old, which I have stored up for you, my beloved.*

Pictures Of You

Keep a nice, attractive picture of your spouse in your car and workplace. The picture will help keep your spouse on your mind. After looking at the pictures throughout the day, you will find yourself longing for them. When you see them, you will be more enthusiastic about them being around, which will help your spouse feel cared for. Looking at family pictures occasionally during the day helps triage our thinking. *TRIAGE (Task Requiring Important Activities Go Early)* prioritizes our day from most to least important. We break up the day's stress by having pleasant thoughts and focusing on what is truly important. Our families are why we work and strive to complete the most challenging tasks. Once your mental break ends, dive back enthusiastically to finish your work and return home to the important ones.

The picture your spouse carries of you has a significant meaning to them. There are specific feelings attached to the picture, which contains something they *LIKE (Love Instills Kind Emotions)* about you. Perhaps it's how you smile and remember when you were happy, or they loved how you looked when you took better care of yourself. When you see them carrying a picture, determine what they like about that particular photo. The person in that photo is who they love and want us to be. Often, what they are looking at is something we have lost, so we may need to work on being that person again so we will never be far from their thoughts.

Psalm 143:8 Cause me to hear your loving kindness in the morning, for I trust in you. Cause me to know the way in which I should walk, for I lift up my soul to you

Kindness

Have you ever thought about doing something for your spouse, like cooking their favorite meal or buying something they like, but hesitated only to have your spouse later say how long it's been since they had the very thing you were thinking of? Sometimes, God places prompts in our hearts based on our spouse's innermost desires. Why? Because He is trying to teach us how to love them. Maybe you don't know how to show love the way your spouse wants to be loved, but God does so follow His lead. You have an inner voice of ideas called **PROMPTS (Pushes Received Outside Me Persuading Their Start)**. These are not just thoughts. They are indications that we sometimes understand our spouses' desires even when they don't show us any signals.

If you think about doing something for or with your spouse, God is nudging you to take action. Don't let the opportunities **PASS (Put A Safe Space)** you by to show love. However, your heart prompts you in more than just your relationships. There may be helpful and healthy things you think of doing for yourself or an unfinished project you decide to work on just before someone asks you about it. Following your internal prompts brings subconscious information to the forefront of our minds. The more you follow, the better prepared you will be to be successful in relationships and life.

1 Kings 19:12 After the earthquake a fire passed;
but Yahweh was not in the fire.
After the fire, there was a still small voice.

Walk By Faith

You got married by faith, believing you would be together forever. We have faith that we can live up to the things in our vows to overcome obstacles and that our feelings won't change. We didn't enter thinking we would fail; faith in our ability got us into a marriage. Now, we need faith in God to stay married. Sometimes, problems get so bad that you may no longer love each other enough to stay together. However, when the love for your spouse runs out, your love for family and God gives you enough faith to try again. *FAITH (Forsaking All I Trust Him)* holds it together when things go wrong and you no longer feel like being married. Your commitment to God first, then to your spouse, can sustain any marriage if you let it. As long as you believe in yourselves, you will be unstoppable.

Faith at work is an essential ingredient to any successful endeavor. Faith isn't just believing; it is working towards what you believe in with great effort. Faith means striving to *WORK (What Objectives Require Keeping)* it out. Every time someone speaks against your actions, faith doesn't accept their lack of confidence. Faith is the source of confidence you need to turn difficult situations around. You must believe in your skills and that you will see change if you work and wait. Sometimes, you have to have faith that things will turn around for your spouse and your home. Just remember, if you believe it, you can receive it.

James 2:18 Yes, a man will say, "You have faith, and I have works." Show me your faith without works, and I will show you my faith by my works.

Man In The Mirror

Every experience and event in our life is filtered through our understanding of it and interpreted based on our optimistic, pessimistic, or realistic **OUTLOOK (Our Unique Take Leave Out Other Knowledge).** These are not emotions but ways of thinking that lead to our possession of a positive, negative, or neutral attitude. Optimism and realism are stable personality traits. One may think that realism is preferred overall, but realism, in this sense, is inactive. It merely accepts circumstances without hope or fear and limits potential. Optimism expects good rather than evil and has positive physical and mental health benefits that help us become better emotionally adjusted and more successful.

Don't create a negative or a neutral when you can have a positive. **OPTIMISM (Opportune Positive, Tenacious Intimate Moments I Stand Motivated)** doesn't mean that you are out of touch but that you focus on what you can and can't control and work for what's best. Positivity causes you to speak and behave in a manner that honors your spouse, giving truthful compliments, valuable encouragement, and growth. It brings peace and security to your home, creating an atmosphere conducive to healthy thoughts and joyful experiences. Please do your best to hope and think positively so it latches on and becomes contagious in your marriage.

Philippians 4:8 Finally, brothers, whatever things are true, whatever things are honorable, whatever things are just, whatever things are pure, whatever things are lovely, whatever things are of good report: if there is any virtue and if there is anything worthy of praise, think about these things.

California Dreamin'

An adage, "The honest miller has a golden thumb," was based on rubbing cornflower between the thumb and forefinger to judge its quality, eventually leading to using the term green thumb for those with a talent for gardening. A green thumb describes those who cultivate things for growth so they don't wither and *DIE (Departure Into Eternity)*. At one time, learning how to grow things to feed your family was necessary for a stable life. It is a skill anyone can learn and will determine whether you strive or truly *THRIVE (Therapeutic Healing Really Is Valued Encouragement)*. We aren't doing this for nothing; we expect a good return. Your marriage is in your hands; how you rub it together shows its quality. So, gain skills and have a green thumb.

Be a *GARDENER (Growing A Rejuvenating Dream Environment Nurturing Earthly Reward)* for your marriage. Plant a seed in the right environment to foster its nature to become more than it currently is. The same things you do to that plant for it to grow, you need to do for your marriage. Water your plant, providing for its needs, and put it in the sun by going out regularly with your spouse. Fertilize it by doing things to keep your relationship healthy. Prune your plant, cutting off everything damaging, and pull up the weeds surrounding it that cause it harm. Talk to it, give some TLC, building your marriage on optimistic hope and words. Enjoy that it's no longer a seed but something you have grown. If you know how to care for a seed, you will find out that you have a flower.

John 15:1 I am the true vine, and my Father is the farmer.

Forever Young

Your spouse's stories about their childhood make up what shaped them from a child to an adult. We should not lose these critical events but write them down so that future generations will know who they were and the importance of their values and actions. Listen when they tell you about when they were a **CHILD (Core Honesty Igniting Long Desire)**. Use the information to support them and not to tear them down. If your spouse passes first, you will have the stories to tell the great-grandchildren about your spouse and you.

You want to do something personal and memorable. Find out if your spouse ever had a disappointing moment where there was something they always wanted but never got. If it is reasonable based on their current maturity, **WAIT (Will Answer In Time)** a little while, and then get it for them. They may love it. There may be things that they would no longer want, like a **CHEMISTRY (Charm Has Enticed My Interest Show Thoughts Regarding You)** set, but you could make a passport with tickets stating, "My Chemistry Set," taking them to a science museum. Each page in their passport booklet is an activity you will see and do to awaken and fulfill their old desires. Rent the old model car they wanted and drive for a day. Purchase the vintage doll and host a tea party. Make it memorable for them, and it will be unique for you.

Deuteronomy 4:9 Only be careful, and keep your soul diligently, lest you forget the things which your eyes saw, and lest they depart from your heart all the days of your life; but make them known to your children and your children's children.

Night Moves

Night freedom is typically the first sign that we have moved from adolescence to adulthood. We pushed our parents and guardians to see if we could stay out later to have fun and as a sign of responsibility. There is no couple's curfew; when together, you should hang out as much as you want, but you don't want to make hanging out late without your spouse a regular habit. Parents and relatives limited the time we stayed out until we could prove our maturity. They worried about us when we took too long or didn't communicate any technical issues, causing delays. We went out like pilots, only to find our flight grounded because of misconduct and miscommunication. Just as our families were home worrying about us, our spouses may also **WORRY (Waiting On Responsible Reasons Yourself)**.

An occasional girls' or guy's night is okay, but too much of it will divide you. As with anything, moderation is always the rule. Staying out **LATE (Limiting Arriving Tardy Expected)** alone or with friends causes insecurity. Your spouse expects the same maturity and responsibility as your parents or guardians once did. Late nights increase the risk of adultery, substance abuse, arrest, and accidental death. Just as you worry about your children, your spouse worries about you. When you stay out late, they stay up late. So, get home soon and get some sleep.

Isaiah 5:11 Woe to those who rise up early in the morning, that they may follow strong drink, who stay late into the night, until wine inflames them!

My Stress

Whether you're a dual-career couple or have a single working spouse, stress is a reality of everyday work. Both require empathy and understanding to lessen the effects of **STRESS (Someone Tries Repairing Every Situation Solo)** on the family. Learning about your spouse's occupation and work environment gives clues to the stresses they come home with and hints at how not to trigger a wrong response after a bad day at work. Understanding what they are going through helps us not get offended if they come home with an attitude, and it gives us the wisdom to know how to change their demeanor. Resilience comes from being good at managing **STRESS (Senseless Turmoil Requiring Emotionally Sensible Solutions)**. Helping your spouse to relax and take time to destress improves the strength of the marriage.

A stressed spouse is a stressed house. **STRESS (Strong Tendencies Resist Effective Spiritual Solutions)** comes from unsure responses. Many tend to give solutions without listening, but a listening ear is the first thing we can do to help our spouse de-stress. They need to get it off their chest. It may seem like they are unloading a heavy burden onto you, but seek to help, not take it personally. After listening, please offer support and seek to coach, not correct them. Coaching uses fundamentals to build strength, while correction points out weaknesses. You may have to gently shift their focus from work to home to help them decompress from the stress.

*Proverbs 12:25 Anxiety in a man's heart weighs it down,
but a kind word makes it glad.*

Legs

Our first look drew most of us to our spouse. Something was appealing about them even if we recognized and ignored it. Whatever it was that we liked, attractiveness goes much deeper. Relationships built on outer appearance are shallow and sketchy. You can't build a good relationship on pretty but petty. Others will let you know how handsome or beautiful you are, but your spouse cares much more about how good you look on the inside. Spend as much on making yourself attractive inside as you have been working on the outside. Being ***ATTRACTIVE (Alluring Temptation That Receives A Compliment They're Indeed Visibly Enchanting)*** is not only about the externals but what they receive from inside of you.

Men tend to want peace, pleasure, partnership, and passion in their women, and women want security, support, strength, and straightforward-ness in men. The way you treat them is the most attractive quality. Outer beauty catches the eye; inner beauty captures the heart. Everyone else may ***COMPLIMENT (Catching Our Most Pleasant Likable Intimate Moments Ensures Nice Thoughts)*** your spouse on the exterior things like their looks, but you compliment them by your character. Having a spouse with thought-ful behavior is its own reward. Putting a little makeup on your personality will make them think you are beautiful/handsome through and through.

1 Peter 3:34 Let your beauty come not from the outward adorning of braiding your hair, and of wearing gold ornaments or of putting on fine clothing, but from the hidden person of the heart, in the incorruptible adornment of a gentle and quiet spirit, which is very precious in God's sight.

ABC

Learning is an ongoing process in life. People love learning new facts, but facts that aren't applied are useless. We should keep learning **FACTS (Firm Accurate Clues Teach Something)**, but we also need to learn new skills. Acquiring knowledge is fun, but skills are more helpful. Every new skill you learn has something in it that you can apply to your marriage. Learning a new skill means you have goals, motivation, and focus. It also means you take steps to get out of your comfort zone. These are superior qualities that allow you to learn a new skill and build the character and quality of your marriage. Learning skills is not about the task but about self-development. It's taking the limits off your current predicament and opening up new opportunities.

Skills break down into life skills for everyday practice, such as cooking skills, learning the internet, or even auto mechanics, and professional development skills, such as interpersonal relationships, leadership, and administrative skills to assist in achieving your goals. Whether it's the critical thinking skills you learn from mathematics, learning business and administrative skills, or something related to your profession. Each **SKILL (Strategic Knowledge Igniting Lasting Learning)** you learn helps your household. When you learn new skills, you can combine them creatively, leading to success. Each time you learn something new, talk about it with your spouse. They may add to what you have learned.

Proverbs 22:29 Do you see a man skilled in his work? He will serve kings. He won't serve obscure men.

The Climb

Whenever we are in a close relationship, we will face challenges. Our habits, attitudes, and values make relationships attractive and aggravating. We each face things that are difficult to deal with in the other. However, people do not respond well to those who try to force change on them. Seek growth in them, not change, because we only **CHANGE (Choosing Honesty Allows New Growth Everyday)** mistakes. People who try to change for the sake of change don't see the changes they want to make. When we seek to grow, the changes in our hearts, minds, and attitudes keep pace. Growth isn't selective about changing one thing and ignoring others. Growth focuses on maturity. People respond to what makes them grow, not who wants them to change. You don't need to change them. You need to help/allow them to grow.

We must realize that the difference you have seen in your life has been from growth rather than someone trying to change you. The spouse you seek is a **MATURE (Mellow Appreciation To Unleash Relational Endurance)** version of their current self. You can help them grow by accepting them with the kindness and compassion that will make them want to grow. We should be the change we want to see in the world and our relationships. Take it slow, and don't try to force change in your spouse; instead, seek to grow together.

2 Thessalonians 1:3 We are bound to always give thanks to God for you, brothers, even as it is appropriate, because your faith grows exceedingly, and the love of each and every one of you toward one another abounds.

God's Got A Blessing

The Covid 19 recession made the rich richer by making suitable investments in a down market. Business-oriented individuals expanded their normal operations by finding and selling goods others needed, but they usually don't sell. It was supply and demand at its finest. As demand increased, so did prices. At the same time, the poor and unprepared struggled and hoarded resources for a rainy day. Some who were overextended lost their properties, and many inherited others' belongings and sought to sell them quickly. Those who had saved and maintained good **CREDIT (Confidence Related Earns Double In Trials)** scores found opportunities to purchase properties at a discount.

Recessions are unexpected but happen repeatedly. No matter how far away, be **READY (Resources Expected Are Deemed Yours)** for the next opportunity. Prepare for the next recession by saving all you can and paying your bills on time. Many people who took advantage were not business savvy. Still, because they were ready for a rainy day, they had the opportunity to snatch up properties and items that were now available to them. Rainy day savings can mean you are ready for a rainbow. When the next recession comes, you can buy cheap-income property and leave an inheritance for your children.

Luke 19:13 He called ten servants of his and gave them ten mina coins, and told them, 'Conduct business until I come.

You've Been So Faithful

Deeds are actions and more. They speak of triumphs and who we are as a person. A deed is also a word on paper that declares your ownership. Symbolically, it means our deeds are about taking ownership of our responsibilities. The words we exchanged at our wedding established our marriage, but we had to follow it up with deeds. These words are promises we must keep or lose our credibility. The promises outlined your vows, and we expect the **DEEDS (Determined Energetic Efforts Done Supportively)** to be faithful to those very same vows. Our basic promises are to be consistent, considerate, comforting, and cooperative, and we should make every attempt to make our deeds commensurate.

We show faithfulness when we link our actions to our words. A good person does good deeds regardless of the size of the audience. Even if no one sees your deeds, they give us a sense of accomplishment. Consistency between our words and **ACTIONS (Activity Can Triumph If Operation Needs Strength)** influences our friends and inspires others to be better people. They leave an invisible trail imprinted in the hearts of our children. Sometimes, our deeds accompany our words; other times, the deed speaks for us. Our deeds tell us where our hearts are at. To trust you, they have to trust your word and character. Start looking to do one good deed daily, keep consistent, and witness the results.

Daniel 11:32 He will corrupt those who do wickedly against the covenant by flatteries; but the people who know their God will be strong and take action.

Forgive Them Father

When someone does us **WRONG (What Reproaches Our Normal Guidelines)**, we usually want them to pay, so what's the price for your forgiveness? You may think that's silly and that you don't have a price and only struggle to forgive. Many of us haven't considered it, but that struggle has a repayment plan or a level of suffering they must endure to satisfy you. Your place of satisfaction is the price you place on forgiveness, So I ask again, "How High is the Price of your Forgiveness?" Forgiveness can be difficult because unrequited or unpaid forgiveness costs us our pride. We often require something in exchange for releasing the person with an attitude while preserving our pride. Free forgiveness kills self-pride, and keeping pride is often more important to some than healing in their hearts.

FORGIVE (Former Objections Receive Grace Instilling Verified Exoneration) your spouse quickly. You pay the price for holding onto unforgiveness that affects your health, emotions, and freedom. Do not hold on to your problems for so long. Quick resolution and forgiveness will allow you freedom in marriage. Many diseases are stress-related because of unforgiveness and frustration. They are the actual price of unforgiveness. It hurts you, and it kills your marriage. Whatever happens, seek to forgive because the price of holding on is too high.

Matthew 5:25 Agree with your adversary quickly while you are with him on the way; lest perhaps the prosecutor deliver you to the judge, and the judge deliver you to the officer, and you be cast into prison.

I Won't Complain

Complain to others about yourself, not your spouse. Half the people we complain to wont help, and nearly the other half are glad you have problems. We focus too much on what our spouses are not. If you tell people about your relationship, tell them about your shortcomings, not only those of your spouses. You have **FAULTS (Flaws Are Unattended, Leaving Terrible Shortcomings)** and are the only one who can fix them. We see more improvement when we work on ourselves than when we work on others. Never tell anyone anything private unless they are both willing and able to help both of you.

Spouses should hear more compliments than they do complaints. When you complain harshly to your spouse, they go into defense mode, which shuts down good communication. People who rarely complain regularly overlook faults and deserve an apology when they do because that means you did something to hurt them. We must base our apologies on truth and **REGRET (Reasons Enabling Greif Reflect Extreme Trauma)**. When the action wasn't wrong but negatively impacted someone, it's okay to show kindness because of the offense but stand on the truth. Consistent complainers rarely overlook faults, and apologizing to them all the time may do more harm than good. Even when they are wrong, they complain, and when we apologize to calm their anger, it cements their attitude.

Isaiah 32:17 The work of righteousness will be
peace, and the effect of righteousness,
quietness and confidence forever.

Don't Be Cruel

Don't be cruel is not just an Elvis song; it's a word for the wise. If you have a difficult day or resent someone, deal with it before you deal with others. You do not want to take it out on your family. You must maintain a proper attitude and not be rude when you're not in the mood. Rude behavior may get you what you want if that's to be left alone. However, your spouse may have resentment when you no longer feel that way. Being **RUDE (Rough, Unhappy, Disagreeable Events)** often works to shut down a conversation that causes others to drop the issue. It quickly boosts self-esteem, but it doesn't last. You often have to deal with the consequences even when you don't remember why. Rude jokes are funny because of the punchline, but make sure your family doesn't feel like a punchline when they talk to you.

Being authentic doesn't mean you have to be rude. Rudeness affects the peace of your home. Rude responses practice negativity. Sometimes, we show rudeness when kindness would have been more appropriate. Rudeness doesn't show strength; it masks deep-seated resentment and weakness. It is a sign of insecurity, inability to communicate appropriately, and a lack of character. You attract more flies with **HONEY (Hope Our Nectar Entices You)** than you do with vinegar. Be respectful, and the people will give you your time alone without the ill feelings that come with rudeness.

Proverbs 12:18 There is one who speaks rashly like the piercing of a sword, but the tongue of the wise heals.

Stand By Me

As Dolly Parton put it, "Stand by Your Man," the same applies to men to stand by their women. You are to be their strength when they are weak, protection when attacks come, and stability when everything goes wrong. When we **STAND** *(Stay True And Never Deviate)* by them, they know they are not alone or abandoned. We become the staff they lean on, lifting them. We all remember when we felt someone should protect us but didn't. Being **UNPROTECTED** *(Under No Protection, Risk Of Trouble Exists Caution Taken Ensures Defense)* can scar our thoughts and cause more significant relationship insecurities.

Not only do we stand by our spouses, but we must also stand **UP** *(Uniting People)* for them. Our spouses may offend someone by doing something that wasn't wrong, but someone disliked. If someone comes against your spouse, you must stand up for them firmly. Not by throwing blows or having an adult tantrum, but by standing between your spouse and attacker and letting them know you don't tolerate disrespect towards them. Standing up for them will make a deep impression on your spouse, making them more likely to **DEFEND** *(Dedication Enter Fight Ending Negative Demeanors)* you. You may have to put your reputation and some relationships on the line, but your family is worth it. We should publicly defend them but privately correct them if they are wrong.

Psalm 91:14 Because he has set his love on me, therefore I will deliver him. I will set him on high, because he has known my name.

Like A Prayer

Often, we tell our spouses we pray for them daily, but they don't see it. **GRAB (Go Right About Boldly)** their hand and pray to God for them on the spot. If they are going through something, increase your prayer by calling them and leaving prayers on their voicemail. Text them after you pray to let them know they are in your thoughts. Couples' prayer is a way of supporting spouses by building on their faith. It shows thoughtfulness and encourages them to expect better when enduring hardships. The more they see you do it, the more significant concern they feel you show for them. However, what you pray must be consistent with what you believe and how you live your life.

PRAYER (People Request As Yahweh Expects Repentance) isn't just asking things from God. It is not about receiving as much as it is relating. An all-knowing God doesn't need prayer to act. We need prayer to acknowledge and gain a more intimate knowledge of Him. Prayer draws us closer, and as you hear your prayers, you should determine how to make the changes under your control and trust God to do the rest. When we pray for restoration, we should work on it. We must get up and make better decisions if we are interceding for our finances. We do our part in **PRAYER (Position Requiring A Yielded Ear Respond)**.

Daniel 6:10 When Daniel knew that the writing was signed, he went into his house (now his windows were open in his room toward Jerusalem) and he kneeled on his knees three times a day, and prayed, and gave thanks before his God, as he did before.

California King

Have you ever seen a couple out on a date, and all they do is look at their phones? That's how we look when we play games on our phones, use social media, work, or watch TV in bed with our spouse. Your **BEDROOM (Base Ending Days Restfully Once Obstacles Move)** is not for other things that are not about you. For years, my wife insisted that we not have a television in our bedroom, which led to us expressing more thoughts and feelings toward each other. TV or Computers in the bedroom at night may help you wind down or get extra work done, but they kill conversations. Unless you're watching a show you both enjoy, turn the TV off and do not use social media in bed. They take the focus off each other, placing more interest and involvement in the show than in your spouse. Take it somewhere else.

Enjoy late-night conversations or games. Make the bedroom about the two of you and not everyone else. Our Bedroom is a sanctuary of relaxation where we rest, recuperate and regroup. It is where we can kiss our spouse goodnight every night. It's a retreat after the kids have gone to bed. The bed is where we can discuss the moments, laugh with each other, and show our love beyond our words. It is the place most want to be when they pass from this world. Keep your bedroom as an **OASIS (Our Attitude Shows Intense Stability)**, and you will find peace in paradise.

Songs of Solomon 1:4 Take me away with you. Let's hurry. The king has brought me into his rooms. Friends We will be glad and rejoice in you. We will praise your love more than wine! Beloved They are right to love you.

Pleasure, Little Treasure

A successful Christian marriage establishes a spiritual connection by putting God first and seeking His strategic guidance in dealing with matters of family and life. Our order of priorities starts with God, each other, children, work, ministry, friends, and extended family. Though we sacrifice for our spouses, we won't be much good for them if we don't *CARE (Civil Actions Require Encouraging)* for ourselves. I use ministry because the church is about being strengthened in fellowship and service and is a way to connect spiritually with God. Still, it is not the connection in totality. The Lord will judge the way you talk to and treat your spouse. I don't know about you, but when we get to heaven, if some of us make it, many of our crowns will be lopsided because of all the attitude we have given our spouse.

Store up treasures in heaven by treating your spouse with kindness and honor. *TREASURE (Timeless Resources Esteemed As Select Unique Riches Encountered)* them loving, appreciating, and forgiving them. Show them humility, patience, and how kind you can be so you can work in unity. Sometimes, we know what right to do but don't do it. When we spend time with God, He will help us balance ourselves and consider our spouse a valuable part of our lives. What you value, you treasure, so make God first and treasure your spouse. It's God's way.

Matthew 6:20-21 But lay up for yourselves treasures in heaven, where neither moth nor rust consume, and where thieves don't break through and steal; for where your treasure is, there your heart will be also.

Blessing On Blessing (B.O.B Bounce)

We hear so much from couples about their struggles and striving to survive, but what about talking about their success? Some couples are doing amazing things and enjoying life together. Talk with them and discover what they are doing that is working and what they have learned from their failed attempts. Everything helps. We don't just need advice when things are going wrong; advice on improving a good relationship is also beneficial. Bounce ideas off of other married couples of things you can do to improve your marriage. Men go to other faithfully married men and share what made their spouse go, "Wow, Honey" (nothing private). Women do the same. Use their fresh ideas to make your marriage a moment maker.

Every marriage is different, so don't try to imitate their actions; instead, use similar ideas that you modify to fit your marriage modality. Sometimes, the best self-help book is the person you have admired. Faithful, committed couples can **HELP (Hope Encourages Lifting People)** other faithful committed couples. Ask about dating ideas, time management ideas, and helpful tips that they encounter. You may even want to give another couple a copy of this book to **TIP (Topple Into Position)** things in their favor. Remember, relationships last because we handled the hard times with love and consideration and squeezed the most out of the good times.

Ecclesiastes 9:9 Live joyfully with the wife whom you love all the days of your life of vanity, which he has given you under the sun, all your days of vanity, for that is your portion in life, and in your labor in which you labor under the sun.

Manolo

You have a NIL look and should have a NIL attitude. **NIL** stands for **Name, Image, and Likeness**. We must establish our walk with God and carry His name with integrity and character. God creates man and woman to reflect His Image and portray His Likeness. God's first purpose for marriage wasn't productivity or procreation; it was to reflect His image through nurturing love and unity. However, neither can reflect the fullness of God's image without being united. Marriage fully describes what it means to operate in God's image. Recognizing that God's **IMAGE (If My Appearance Grows Effectively)** is the primary purpose of your marriage permits us to focus on implementing changes that allow us to portray a clearer picture of the Lord through understanding and forgiving each other

A **NIL (Need Image Likeable)** attitude keeps our focus on how we act, operate, and what we accomplish. God makes us in His likeness, which means we can take the limits off of who we are and show our spouses a glimpse of what God is like. Great marriages reflect the character and strength of God. Wrong acts mar the image of God, and good ones bring out His likeness in us. Though it can be a struggle, you and your spouse have the innate ability to become unified in everything you set your mind to. The power of a unified front in prayer, finances, and issues will always reflect God's victorious likeness in you.

Genesis 1:27 God created man in his own image.
In God's image he created him;
male and female he created them.

Step Up

During most of my marriage, it seemed that I was the good, the forgiving, and the one who strived to do the most. We both worked, but I was the one who got up with the babies at night, did the laundry, paid the bills, and cleaned a little more than she did. Yeah, she had many pressures, as she was a great organizer who handled children's conferences, events, and other things well. I thought of myself as the brainy one, but I lacked the temperance to keep myself calm when the kids didn't get their homework right. I judged my acts as putting more in than she did because my efforts seemed more valuable than her contributions. I didn't consider that because my job was more flexible, allowing me to make my hours fit right for us to do more things. When I had a season where I was doing everything she did, I realized how tough she was and how bad I was at **DOING (Duty Opposition Is Not Good)** them.

I judged what I did as more essential and felt I worked harder, yet I realized that she was the one growing and healing from her issues, and I was not. Even if I started doing more, she surpassed me, and I lagged. I had to **STEP UP (Striving To Elevate Purposefully Until Progress)** and realize that my opinion about who does the most was based on my focus on the discomforts endured and not on the mutual things we shared. Reevaluate and realize that your efforts may not be the most significant consideration; perhaps they do more than you give credit for.

Proverbs 18:17 He who pleads his cause first seems right
— until another comes and questions him.

My Sacrifice

Most marriages have at least one individual giving more than the other. It would be fantastic if both individuals in marriage were givers and even better if there were sacrificers'. Sacrifice picks up where giving ends. Someone can be a giver of things that don't matter much to them. However, sacrifice is always giving up what is valuable. Sacrifice means giving up your interest for the greater good of a relationship or someone else. *SACRIFICE (Selfless Actions Cause Reparations If Forces In Conflict Erupts)* in marriage doesn't mean you don't get what you want, but it is about putting your spouse's needs on an equal level and deciding whose needs will come first. It's not healthy to always be the only one sacrificing, as it will build regret in you and selfish expectations in your spouse.

Love reveals our ability to give when it hurts, yet it is more about joy-giving than pain. Success requires treating our sacrifices as investments for a better future. Sacrifice can lead to more robust, honest, and joyful relationships. A healthy marriage will contain a level of mutual sacrifice, and caring for our relationships is a form of self-care. Where we live, our time, energy, and our *KNACK (Keep Near Acquired Core Knowledge)* for always being right are things that it may be essential to give up in relationships. Every sacrifice you make should be a choice for a better future. So don't be afraid to sacrifice for your marriage and gain new strength.

Romans 12:1 Therefore I urge you, brothers, by the mercies of God, to present your bodies a living sacrifice, holy, acceptable to God, which is your spiritual service.

Lyin' Eyes

Few things destroy a marriage, quite like adultery. It is an act of betrayal that robs your spouse of what belongs to them. It is hard to deal with because broken trust leaves pain. No matter how much they love you, women generally react with pain and struggle with how little they mean to you, leading to repeated questioning regarding how this ever occurred and what to do about it. Men generally react with pride and struggle to remain in a relationship where they are not honored. Adultery is a term dealing with corruption. To adulterate means adding an **IMPURE (Imperfect Mixture Polluting Unity Reflects Errors)** element to a masterpiece. We must see our marriages as masterpieces placed together. Anything added to your masterpiece that doesn't belong is an unclean element.

Adultery occurs in the head long before it happens in the bed. Exes, porn, and people who fill physical and emotional needs that are to be met by your spouse are unclean to you. We must stop them in our minds because when we enjoy them, the only thing that stops adultery is a lack of opportunity. A moment of pleasure can lead to a lifetime of pain that it is never worth. You lose the respect of your spouse, and when your children no longer see you as who they thought you were, it's nearly impossible to recover. **Fire (Flames Igniting Restricted Emotions)** burns, so put it out quickly and don't play with it in your mind; it only leads to destruction.

Proverbs 6:32 He who commits adultery with
a woman is void of understanding.
He who does it destroys his own soul.

Hold Onto Me

I believe you should live the best life, your high life, all within your married life. We shouldn't disparage single life, thinking everyone should be married. Singles can live a very fulfilling life. However, marriage is the family's foundation and cornerstone of a strong society. Married **LIFE (Live In Full Effect)** causes you to think and act differently than when you were single. We are relational beings, and the most robust form of relationship we see reflected on earth is having a good marriage, which takes some work to build. Married life is a journey a couple navigates as they steer and power the ship together. It is the hope of growing old, raising offspring, cooperating, investing love, nurturing, structure, and values into your children.

Your marriage is your life. It involves all aspects of it. It is sharing your **JOURNEY (Jotting Our Unique Route Navigates Exploring Yourself)** with a good friend and lover, enjoying it, and reaching your destination together. It's not a me thing. To use a little slang, it's a we thang. Two people becoming one required leaving things behind and pressing forward together against all opposition. This type of unity affects your job, family, friends, hobbies, and habits. Your marriage changes everything, but change is good. Your life is no longer about you. It's about our ability to work and enjoy things together.

Jeremiah 29:6 Take wives and father sons and daughters. Take wives for your sons, and give your daughters to husbands, that they may bear sons and daughters. Multiply there, and don't be diminished.

Bridge Over Troubled Waters

Great solutions come from working together. Confusion only comes from working independently of your spouse. You can overcome any problem together, but if you work alone, you become part of the problem. Life is not math; several ways exist to *SOLVE (Solutions Organized Logically Verify Explanations)* our problems. Asking yourself the core of the problem and addressing how to fix it should be agreed upon. Couples are not looking for a good solution, but they are looking for the best one for all. Even a good solution that ignores your spouse may meet with opposition.

Often, couples address the symptoms of their problems rather than the cause. Being unsatisfied with your spouse may not change with more dating or time together if the real problem is a loss of purpose or identity. We must ask ourselves why we feel, respond, or act this way to resolve the core issue. Finding out what decisions opened the door to the problem and discussing how to close them is cardinal. If the doors aren't closed, another problem will arise. *SOLVE (Strategy Of Limiting Vague Experience)* problems with future productivity in mind. Realize that our spouses see things we don't and have ideas we haven't thought about. Let's stop avoiding conflict as our spouse pushes us to take a stand. Engage, control, and solve all your problems together.

Ecclesiastes 4:9 Two are better than one,
because they have a good reward for their labor.

Bills, Bills, Bills

Financial conflict is the number one stressor in marriages. We eradicate our peace and security when the bills start piling up. This is especially true when one spouse handles the bills but hides how bad the situation is from the other, allowing them to spend without considering the bills they didn't know they had. No one likes **BILLS (Basic Invoice Listing Liabilities Spent)**, but they are essential to stay ahead of. Staying ahead is about maintaining financial control of your life. A little paycheck planning will help you focus on spending only on what you need so you can use the leftover money to pay your bills. Prioritize your spending by focusing on your needs rather than your wants or desires. Most debt comes from doing the things we desire but do not need, so take a period of foregoing spending on wants and desires so that you can chip away at your bills.

Deposit your money right away and pay the necessary bills. Revisit your budget whenever you get a little behind in your bills. Search the internet for suggestions on how to lower your expenses. **DEBT (Doing Everything Brings Trouble)** is a trap that's easy to fall into and hard to escape. How we eat and entertain can easily cost most couples a few hundred bucks a month, which could have gotten them out of debt. The goal is to get out of debt and stay three months ahead on bills by building our savings. Stay calm and keep climbing, and you will find your way out.

*Luke 14:28 For which of you, desiring to build
a tower, doesn't first sit down and
count the cost, to see if he has enough to complete it?*

Just The Way You Are

We should work to keep our spouse interested in us. The best way to keep someone interested is by finding out what initially attracted them to you and doing those things. However, the flip side is that we must do whatever it takes also to find a way to stay interested in our spouses. People stray when they find interest or emotional support in other things. These are the things that we are to have in our spouse. What things **GAINED (Getting An Increase, Netting Earnings Due)** your interest in the first place? Looking for and letting our spouses know what they are helps us focus on our spouses. Interest in our spouse motivates us to maintain our commitment.

Our focus makes us say no to convenient things and stick with what we are committed to. No one should show our spouse more **INTEREST (Intense Notice That Enthusiastically Rises Everytime Something Tempts)** than we do. Prove to them that you genuinely are focused on them before someone else pulls them away. Kiss and hug them every morning and evening, and remind them of your love daily. When they call, you respond with **ENTHUSIASM (Energy Needed To Have Unbridled Strength Is Always Spiritually Motivated)** so they will know you are happy to hear from them. When you see them, they will meet you with anticipation. When they come home, don't throw the baby at them; stop what you are doing and hug them. Make them feel that their presence makes your day better.

*Ephesians 5:33 Nevertheless each of you must
also love his own wife even as himself;
and let the wife see that she respects her husband.*

Always And Forever

Some businesses give longevity bonuses to those who work in a position or a company for a long time. Longevity is a recognition and reward for a continued commitment. Longevity in Marriage is a great thing. We applaud special anniversaries, giving them names such as the 10th being tin, the 25th silver, 50th gold, the 60th diamond, and the 70th being known as the platinum anniversary. Couples who last to those later anniversaries know how to fall in love with each other daily. They know they either win together or lose everything. A long marriage is a commitment to each other and staying on the same side. We should enjoy our *YEARS (Your Evolving Annual Registered Stages)* together. However, we don't know if they merely exist or if the love is still alive.

Marriage is for life, and the goal is to make it to the end. Kindle the fire of love afresh each day. Do something sweet or silly, but do something to renew your love. Walking or having a cup of coffee with your spouse each day becomes an enjoyable experience when love grows solid. You have that to look forward to if you stick together and build on what you have. Get used to enjoying your spouse today, and you will learn to enjoy them every day. Be lovers and friends, protect *EACH (Enjoying A Complete History)* other, stay devoted, and enjoy each other.

Romans 7:2 For the woman that has a husband is bound by law to the husband while he lives, but if the husband dies, she is discharged from the law of the husband.

Let It Go

Discovering your partner's past during the dating process is essential because it informs you of their temperaments, endurance, and faults so you can get a picture of what is still with them and what they have grown from. Everyone has a past, and once you are married, you should leave their past in the past. The **PAST (Previous Actions Stop Time)** doesn't define or make you, but the present does. If your spouse has a sorted past, be thankful they admitted it, worked on cleaning it up, and became the person you fell in love with. Realize that's not who they are but who they were. Bringing up past failures and mistakes doesn't help anyone.

It's okay to honor the past, but don't lose yourself in it. Leaving the past behind includes moving beyond past hurts and relationships yourself. We do this by reframing our thoughts and relationships with **PAST (Places Attention Stays Tethered)** events. We often frame ourselves as the story's hero, constructing a narrative and placing blame on others without taking ownership of our faults and growing from them. What we don't learn from the past becomes the **FUTURE (Forecast Understanding Tomorrow Usually Reflects Expectations)** we must deal with. Live for what today offers, not what the past has taken. Leave the past before it destroys your future, moving forward and growing stronger from it. Then, you will be ready for the future.

Isaiah 43:18 Don't remember the former things,
and don't consider the things of old.

Beautiful

Knowing your worth is essential to yourself and your marriage. Our sense of **WORTH (We Offer Respect To Honor)** dictates how we are treated and comes from what is inside us. Self-worth based on exterior things is unstable and will fluctuate based on how others talk to and treat you. Never give away your value. People who don't value themselves struggle to find happiness and contentment. Your spouse and children are likely the only intrinsic exteriors you have in your life. They are so close to our hearts that what they say about us affects our feelings or worth the deepest. We can **IGNORE (Individual Generalizing Needs Overlooking Reality Entirely)** all other exteriors, but the thoughts of those closest to us cut the deepest. Each of you is valuable; make sure you appreciate your importance and raise your sense of worth and esteem in your marriage.

We want to **BOOST (Building Others Or Supporting Them)** our self-esteem, not our pride. Self-esteem is a balanced feeling of respect and worth. Pride is self-satisfaction with our abilities, achievements, and activities that lose balance when given too much focus and become arrogant and superior. Pride is not always negative, but its tendency to lose balance is. Self-esteem is positive because it is well grounded in our worth without comparison to others. Help your spouse feel like there is nothing to compare them to. Give realistic compliments and help them understand their value in your family so they keep their esteem and their joy.

Matthew 10:31 Therefore don't be afraid. You are of more value than many sparrows.

Time Capsule

Time capsules contain a cache of information so future people can discover the essential things in our history. Our future family may want to discover things about our time, so make a Marriage Time **CAPSULE (Container Allowing Packaging Something Under Lasting Enclosure)**. You don't have to bury it, but store it away well-labeled. Write letters and place pictures, video files, and marriage artifacts that are important to you in a sealable container. The container doesn't have to be airtight, but you should use plastic covers to preserve things made of paper, like photos and books. Business articles from closed companies can tell them something about your hobbies and habits. Seal it and put it away. Remember those milestone anniversaries tin, silver, gold, diamond, and platinum mentioned in tip one hundred. Pull out your capsule and go through it on those momentous anniversaries.

Each time you **OPEN (One Push Enters Notch)** it, add more to it and never take anything out. After five years, you will forget most of what is in it, so the space in time keeps it fresh and fun. If you have a family tree, you probably want to put it in there for future generations. If you don't have a family tree or record of past relatives, it's a good time to start one. Some companies can help you research them and include stories you have about the people in your genealogy so they survive. Have fun with it. Future generations will appreciate the knowledge it brings.

Deuteronomy 32:7 Remember the days of old.
Consider the years of many generations.
Ask your father, and he will show you; your elders, and they will tell you.

Careless Whispers

Is it your **GOAL (Getting Opportunities And Learning)** to communicate well? Sometimes, we want to be understood better and learn strategies to communicate better. One thing we notice about good communicators is that they use well-thought-out words that clarify what they say without giving any leeway to take their comments out of context. Communication takes patience and practice. Our temptation to respond quickly means we may voice the wrong things, causing a deepening rift. We must struggle not to respond to negative emotions that lead to releasing careless words. When we are defensive, irritated, frustrated, or sad, we may voice things that will affect those closest to us.

CARELESS (Consistently Avoiding Responsibility Encourages Lax Efforts, Slowing Success) means acting as if you care less. Careless words tend to make someone like you less. We waste time and effort trying to make up for something we should never have spoken. Wise people are slow to speak because they know mistakes are costly. Self-control keeps disagreements from becoming arguments. When you practice not speaking harmful things, it becomes easier to withhold your tongue when upset. To be carefree, we cannot be careless. We must use affirming words to help our spouses' character grow. Careless words tear down, so give yourself time to cool down, and never speak out of anger or pain.

Proverbs 15:1 A gentle answer turns away wrath,
but a harsh word stirs up anger.

Magic's In
The Makeup

Time waits for no one. We each will change in one way or another. We can't stop aging, but we can do something to maintain our appearance and remain attractive. Just because we are married doesn't mean we should let ourselves go. Husbands should note sometimes their wives buy lingerie or a new outfit to see if it makes them look attractive to their spouse. Watch when she presents herself like a **FASHION (Fads Adding Style Have Increased Our Notice)** show because it tells you she wants to attract your attention. When men coat themselves with cologne and wear an outfit their wives have noted before they look good, they are purposefully teasing their wife's minds with their looks.

APPEARANCE (A Pretty Presentation Effects Appeal Raising Attraction Needs Constant Effort) matters. If you had to make a first impression on your spouse, would they find you attractive? The answer to that question determines whether you have kept yourself up. If you can't control your weight, don't worry; the shape of your body loses importance over time, but personality always matters. Women who occasionally wear makeup and men who keep neat and trim keep their spouses looking. Your spouse is already attracted, so accentuate your look by wearing clothes and colors that complement your look.

! Peter 3:3-4 Let your beauty come not from the outward adorning of braiding your hair, and of wearing gold ornaments or of putting on fine clothing, but from the hidden person of the heart, in the incorruptible adornment of a gentle and quiet spirit, which is very precious in God's sight.

Hero

Are you up for a **CHALLENGE (Conflict Has Always Left Lasting Experiences Needing Great Energy)**? Because of our competitive nature, people love games and challenges. However, no one likes a challenging relationship. Complicated relationships lead to insecurity, uncertainty, and unneeded stress. Sometimes, we don't know what all the challenges and conflicts are really about. Some have had relationships where they got along but realized the person wasn't the one for them. Now, they are married to the one they wanted and have many challenges and conflicts that they never faced before. Relationships are places for unity and not the place for challenges with each other. Our challenge is to end complications and win our spouses back. How can we do that? Well, think about taking the Love Dare.

I **DARE (Doing A Risky Endeavor)** you to take a risk to gain what you have lost. If you haven't seen the movie Fireproof, watch it with your spouse. It was so influential in challenging marriage unity that a book called The Love Dare emerged from the movie. It is a 40-day discovery on how to love genuinely. It has a one-page lesson on love, daily activity, and reflections. Parts of it are elementary, and other parts are challenging, but it has strengthened many marriages. You may need to take the Love Dare to get your marriage back on track. Doing nothing will help no one. Look into the Love Dare and devote yourselves to it.

Isaiah 50:8 He who justifies me is near. Who will bring charges against me? Let us stand up together. Who is my adversary? Let him come near to me

Oops, I Did It Again

Divorce is never a good thing, but in reality, many couples have divorced and remarried. **DIVORCE (Dissolving Intimate Vows Offers Resentful Couples Exit)** means to divert or separate. You would think that with maturity, the chance of a second or third marriage working would increase, but the chances of divorcing again increase because there are more issues to balance. Many get out of marriages because they refuse to work on themselves or don't take full responsibility, blaming their former spouse for the split. Some do so, possibly intending to remarry one day, but the second marriage requires the same work and commitment they didn't put into the first relationship.

Many people don't do the necessary work between the first and second marriage and carry the same issues into their new relationship. There are ways to increase your chances of success. First, get spiritual counsel or **THERAPY (Talking Has Encouraged Rehab And Positive Yearnings)** to help navigate through old problems and ways of thinking. To reinforce good thinking, have daily devotions together in which you speak about healing actions. Discuss your differences, and then cultivate love to cover them. If you co-parent with your ex, show them respect and demand it for your spouse. This marriage has to be different for it to work. So, take it slow and make sure you have healed.

1 Corinthians *7:15 Yet if the unbeliever departs, let there be separation. The brother or the sister is not under bondage in such cases, but God has called us in peace.*

Put That Woman First

Many people who want to be **FIRST (Foremost Initiator Receives Special Thoughts)** don't want to be the first to forgive or bring peace. We want to be the first in importance, not the first to initiate. The first to initiate often takes a humbler position but deserves the more tremendous honor. They care for what's needed and hold the family and relationship together. Sometimes, one parent initiates activities or things in a child's life more than their spouse, earning a greater appreciation in the child's eyes. We shouldn't think that our children love the other parent more, but they appreciate us differently for what we have done. If we want to be first, we are likely not behaving as the first in serving our family.

Serving your **FAMILY (Family Always Means I Love You)** doesn't make you a pushover but one who has authority and action to do what's best. You have to maintain balance and discipline in the household. The one wanting to be first in the family will not be the most appreciated or rewarded in the voice of their family. That is a particular position for the ones who humble themselves and serve. Families where both parents take equal service roles raise more well-adjusted children. It's a long-term sacrifice to help others reach their potential. People who demand attention will eventually end up with less attention in the eyes of those around them. Those who show attention gain recognition and attention through their intentions.

Mark 9:35 He sat down and called the twelve; and he said to them, "If any man wants to be first, he shall be last of all, and servant of all."

Psalm 23

Contrary to popular opinion, men create life in the womb. Women *NURTURE (Nourishment Unlocks Rapid Transformation Using Regular Encouragement)* the implanted seed, causing it to grow and transform into something extraordinary. Everywhere the husband touches his wife, providing an environment where his wife is safe and can thrive, she will receive his commitment and take and grow it, giving him back more than he has given. Wives will go through hell and high water when they know their husbands love them and keep their best interests at heart. Everywhere you touch your wife, covering her, she touches you back by nurturing strength in that area. She covers you from the inside while you cover her from the outside. The more you secure and protect her, the greater strength she will give you.

Every relationship has three parts. Each portion requires a different aspect and instrument of nurturing. The first *PART (Portion A Route Takes)* is yours, where you nurture your growth through confidence and commitment. The more you mature, the stronger you will be at helping others. The second part belongs to your spouse, where you nurture motivation using understanding and encouragement. Growth is our goal, so give your spouse the same support you desire. The final portion is the relationship; consistency and faithfulness nurture your togetherness. When all is said and done, your spouse stands beside you when your children leave. When we nurture our relationship, we prepare our future.

Ephesians 5:21 subjecting yourselves to one another in the fear of Christ.

Push It To The Limit

Everyone has their limit. Limits are conditions that reduce or restrict us to certain acts. Limits tell us how far we can go before we have to stop. We base our limits on our nature or nurture. Limits based on our nature are things that are humanly impossible to do. Limits based on nurture are things we think we cannot do. Our nature limits humans from flying ourselves, but our nurture has allowed us to fly through the use of innovation. The things we don't accomplish are all things based on the thoughts we have nurtured. Pushing past your limits requires more difficult challenges to reach deferred dreams and goals. You must see where your spouse sets the *LIMIT (Let Intimidation Make Issues Tall)* line and help them push past it.

Helping your spouse *PUSH (Pray Until Something Happens)* past means you may have to endure the hardships that come together. It may get tough, but don't cower; conquer. Push beyond your comfort and convenience and breakthrough. Help encourage them to finish their degree, change your diet with them so they can reach their weight goals, and teach them what you know that will help them in their business or career. Watch your conduct and be supportive because there is a limit to what they will take from you, too. We don't know our actual limits; we limit our thoughts. For many, our previous limit was just the doorway to your next level. Be what they need to break through and surpass all limits.

Philippians 4:13 I can do all things through Christ who strengthens me.

Humble And Kind

When speaking to our spouse, we must realize that not all factual statements are helpful. Some statements are pretty hurtful, so we need to tell the truth with kindness. Rather than speaking critically, sandwich your critique between a positive compliment and an encouragement to improve things. The **COMPLIMENT (Confirmation Of Moderate Praise Leaves Individual Merrily Enjoying Nice Thoughts)** opens your spouse up to listening so they view the following critique as helpful, not condemning. We must base compliments on truth rather than flattery, which fluffs the truth. Critiques are about giving feedback so that someone can change or improve. Following up with encouragement helps your spouse to remain motivated to make the recommended changes due to the critique.

If you want to avoid future mistakes and regrets, think before you speak. Correct as you would your father or mother and not the way you would a child. We often neglect to speak with kindness because getting our point across seems more important to us at the time. We must also speak **KIND (Keep Inspiring Nice Deeds)** to ourselves. Negative self-talk is as destructive as negative spouse talk. Some can praise others but struggle to speak kindly of themselves in their inner thoughts. Start practicing speaking kindly to yourself, your spouse, and your family, and watch love and compassion grow and spread.

1 Kings 12:7 They replied, "If you will be a servant to this people today, and will serve them, and answer them with good words, then they will be your servants forever.

Our House

When we were young, we had to clean our rooms before we went out to play. The principle is ensuring you handle your business at home before doing anything else. Well, it still applies. If your home is not in order when you leave, it will worsen when you return. Putting your house in order is more than cleaning and reorganizing your home. It is taming the chaos in your life by focusing on healthy relational habits based on priorities and responsibilities. **ORDER (Organized Readiness Declutters Every Responsibility)** puts everything in perspective, so we place out-of-order signs on broken things. Our home is out of order when we break promises, miss events, and ignore issues.

STAIRS (Stewardship, Trustworthiness, Accountability, Integrity, Responsibility Sensitivity) represents the six focus areas to place your house in order. Start by handling your financial obligations, and move forward with managing your promises to maintain trust. Our accountability considers others and the input they bring, and integrity makes personal values family values. Focusing on responsibilities keeps us from neglecting any areas that need our attention, and we must remember to be sensitive to the emotional needs in our home. Help your household before you help someone else; you will have peace when you return.

1 Samuel 30:3 When David and his men came to the city, behold, it was burned with fire; and their wives, their sons, and their daughters were taken captive.

Happy

Focusing on the positive aspects of your relationship leads to greater satisfaction. Don't waste time meditating on your partner's faults, flaws, and failures. Your love and commitment are supposed to cover those things. We can mind-bomb ourselves into accepting misunderstanding as facts and perpetuate thoughts that our spouse is against us, even when there is no truth behind it. A *MIND-BOMB (Move In New Direction Because Our Minds Bitterness)* is a thought we integrate that moves contrary to what we know. Brains have a chemical environment that changes based on the way you think. Good thoughts release healthy chemicals that increase joy. Negative thoughts place a damper on the suitable chemicals, leaving our minds in an environment conducive to depression and anxiety.

Your thinking brings you your sunshine or your gloom. You will never see the shadow if you keep your face in the sunshine. Use your thoughts wisely. Part of your brain records good thoughts about your spouse. Another *PART (Portion Allotted Rends Total)* records negative thoughts about them. The part you stay in determines whether your love will shine or you will become self-deceived and despise them. One side will keep you in peace, while the other will break your marriage in pieces. Keeping your mind on the good things will cast negative thoughts away and help you focus and feel better.

Ephesians 4:23 and that you be renewed in the spirit of your mind

Beautiful Day

Men, remember the forget me not calendar where you scheduled when you regularly gave flowers, poems, and gifts? We have already added conversation night, date night & marriage holidays. Now add in a spa day to pamper her. Your **SPA (Supplying Peace Allowed)** day is unique and between just the two of you. No conversation about problems, work, or family is allowed. It's just the two of you. Play relaxing music and use scented candles to provide aromatherapy. Give her a hot oil bath and follow it with a full body massage. End it with a foot massage, and if she is willing, paint her toenails yourself. Ladies, you can do the same, but don't offer to paint his toenails unless it's clear. It can feel a little strange to some men. Top it off with your best meal.

A spa **DAY (Doing Anything Yourself)** There is nothing wrong with having a spa together on a day. Your body is the only place you have to live, so take care of it. Hitting a place with hot mineral springs that can relax and rejuvenate you brings a sense of togetherness. Sometimes, husbands neglect helpful things their wives would **LOVE (Let Others View Emotions)** to do with them because they associate them with girls' activities for their women's day with their friends. Getting beyond your comfort **ZONE (Zeal Offers Needed Energy)** to have a spa day together may be just what you need to open your spouse up and change some routines so you can find deeper enjoyment together.

Proverbs 11:25 The liberal soul shall be made fat.
He who waters shall be watered also himself.

What A Surprise

Everyone loves a surprise party. Surprise adds spice to your life by shocking someone with something they desired but were unprepared for. Surprise your spouse simply for no reason. ***SURPRISE (Sudden Unexpected Recognitions Prompts Reacting In Shocked Expression)*** strengthens your bond and shows your spouse that you are listening and attentive to their desires. You don't have to do anything expensive or elaborate, but you can do something meaningful for them. You can knock something off their bucket list or meet them for a secret rendezvous. If there is something they have always wanted but thought they could accomplish, make an arrangement to experience it. Sometimes, it's as simple as arranging for them to have the alone time they desperately crave.

Surprise your spouse by asking for a special date night, but buy tickets to a concert or sporting event featuring their favorite artist or team. It will be a ***TICKET (Tab Is Certificate Keeping Entrance Time)*** to a good evening and cause them to appreciate their time with you and what you have done. Instead of expecting to come home to see their favorite team on TV or listen to their song, treat them to a live game or performance. Make sure you bring their team jersey or shirt that shows everyone who they are a fan of. They may come as a fan of the team or band, but they will leave as your fan because you gave them a special surprise they wanted.

Proverbs 31:12 She does him good, and not harm, all the days of her life.

I Was Made To Love Her

Have you ever done something without considering what would happen? If you did, you understand that sometimes things go wrong when you don't consider the consequences. Consideration is the habit of careful thinking, evaluating, and weighing options before making decisions. We make considerations to move from bad choices to better ones and from good choices to the best choices. Consideration takes thought weapons out of the hands of those used to wielding them. Even if your people don't like your choice, they will respect that you did **CONSIDER (Contemplation Of New Subjects Involves Directly Examined Response)** them when making it. When you are considered one of the final candidates for a job but don't get it, it gives you confidence that you are qualified, so you approach the following interviews with hope. Consideration works even better in the family.

Showing your spouse consideration tells them they are important to you, which makes all the difference in the world. Instead of feeling dragged along, they will feel comforted. Caring comes from a mind of consideration. You must first consider the worth of something or someone before you *INVEST (Integrated New Ventures Establishes Small Trade)* your heart into it. We can become great lovers if we become great considerers. Consider your God, spouse, and family before acting or making decisions, and you will become more thoughtful and caring.

Philippians 2:4 each of you not just looking to his own things, but each of you also to the things of others.

On The Road Again

Trips can be exhausting and usually require a day or two to recover. Many spouses don't sleep as well away from home because they miss their families and are in unfamiliar surroundings. If your spouse takes a business trip or another trip without you, ensure you take care of everything while they are gone. The *TRIP (Tour Requiring I Plan)* home should not be a more significant worry than the trip away. It takes some additional work for the spouse who remains home, so it's best to start preparation for having the home cleaned, laundry, shopping, and other things done 2 to 3 days before they leave. Since we know when to expect them back, we should have plenty of opportunities to maintain our homes, keep the kids in order, and prepare a warm meal. They should return to a peaceful situation and not to chaos.

Return trips can be rewarding if you prepare for them. Your spouse is glad to return, but sometimes, the one at home is *READY (Recognized Early As Day Yields)* but unprepared. They are so ready to shift responsibilities back to the returning spouse, releasing problems that they don't release attention and affection. We must show them that we missed them more than we missed the help they brought. A prepared spouse allows for downtime because they understand how trips drain us. When the world is in confusion, your home is the place of rescue. Make a plan and keep their return a safe landing.

Luke 8:39 "Return to your house, and declare what great things God has done for you." He went his way, proclaiming throughout the whole city what great things Jesus had done for him.

Who Am I

As couples spend time together, they develop a marriage identity. Marriage identity is the unique thumbprint that evolves as they switch from an I mindset to a we. Marriage **IDENTITY (In Distinguishing Every Nuance To Illustrate That's You)** describes the values, characteristics, and roles the couple falls into that make them the (Whatever your last name is) family. Couples who know their marriage identity have learned to reduce conflict by silently defining certain expectations within their relationship. They call my wife and me the Davises, but it means nothing to us if I don't know my marriage ID. Because they know their family ID, my children may not do some things because they are Davises, and Davises doesn't behave like that. Many families have adopted IDs without even realizing that is what they have done.

Once we know our marriage/family identity, we can strengthen it by discovering what empowers it. It could be love, purpose, convenience, commitment. It would be best if it were a mixture of things, but that is not always the case. If you and your spouse could give a one-word common reason why you married, that is what drives it. You have added other things, but never lose focus on the **DRIVE (Determination Revealed In Versatility Equips)** that motivates you. Determine, reinforce, and build on it for a bulletproof marriage identity.

Genesis 2:23 The man said, "This is now bone of my bones, and flesh of my flesh. She will be called 'woman,' because she was taken out of Man."

Waterfalls

There is a lot of talk about a person's energy these days. Typically, people discuss whether an individual builds and encourages people positively versus someone who drains productivity and mood through negative thoughts and reactions. However, we express it, your **ENERGY (Elevated New Excitement Reactively Generates Youthfulness)** allows others to experience who you are. Additionally, our body's circadian rhythm generally causes us to hours of peak alertness and productivity and times when we taper down. Circadian rhythm doesn't just dictate the time we get sleepy; it is also why some people cannot accomplish much because of losing energy in the early or late afternoon.

In Japan, inemuri is a practice of hardworking employees taking a nap to replenish during low-energy times. Most don't have that luxury and run on empty. Be a spring for your spouse and not a hole that drains them. Being **DRAINED (Diminished Reserves Are Ineffective Need Energizing Daily)** derives from insufficient rest or replenishment. Negativity and overwhelming your spouse with tasks during low-energy hours further drain them. Without energy, your spouse won't be able to give you their all. Be your spouse's advocate. Provide time and find creative ways to make them lie down and rest. You don't have to do it alone when it comes to replenishing them mentally and spiritually. Find ways to get them with people who will strengthen and encourage them so they spring back to life.

Proverbs 5:15 Drink water out of your own cistern,
running water out of your own well.

Take A Fools Advice

Good advice is everywhere, but have you considered why people rarely take it? We meet some people who give us the best advice but don't apply it to their lives. Often, we struggle between the wisdom of advice and the weakness of our will. So, many of us can tell others the right thing to do to fix the same situations we are in but fail to do so ourselves. Following sound *ADVICE (Assistance Determining Victory If Correctly Evaluated)* takes sacrifice that may rob us of feelings of power and pride. We must adjust our attitudes to consider the proper advice for the situation, and there lies the problem. Our mood and outlook about our marital problems often cause us to turn to those who don't make good sounding boards.

People can be your sounding board, giving *FEEDBACK (Fresh Evaluation Eases Drama By Activating Core Knowledge)* or an echo chamber that reflects and amplifies evil thoughts and feelings. When anxious, we rely heavily on advice and need good sources. Talking to everyone about our problems signifies that we want justification, not advice. Avoid causing new problems to family and friends who won't forgive your spouse for what's happening long after you have moved on. Seek counsel from those in healthy, well-balanced marriages who love and support their spouses and understand what you are going through. Keeping the source of advice good can make all the difference you need.

Proverbs 24:6 For by wise guidance you wage your war, and victory is in many advisors

Where Is The Love

Your spouse has dedicated their life, so you **OWE (Others Win Earnings)** them love. There are several types of love. The ancient Greeks used eros, philia, storge, and agape for the first four. The first eros is romantic love, which feeds the passion of our relationship. The second type philia is friendship, a love based on mutual goodwill. The third storge is that we naturally experience familial love within the family between parents and children, which shrinks or grows with experience. The last agape is altruistic love, which seeks the welfare of others and is a willingness to love regardless of the situation. On top of these four, the 5th flirting is a playful enticement built on fun. The 6th is practical love formed by our sense of commitment and duty, with the 7th being self-love based on healthy esteem or corrupted by unbalanced pride.

We must have six of these for our spouse and the seventh balanced for ourselves to embrace all the love marriage has for us. We likely experienced these on our wedding day, creating a new family with the one we loved. When we **DRIFT (Downward Road In Facing Trials)** from our loves, problems arise in our marriage. Love isn't always easy, but working on it is always worth it. Spending time with your spouse working on building interest, intimacy, and integrity will keep you from drifting away. Stay anchored to your spouse and let nothing come between you. Show them all the love you can muster and remain whole as one.

Titus 2:4 that they may train the young wives to love their husbands, to love their children,

The Sweetest Taboo

Don't just get physical; get intimate. Marriage intimacy involves the closeness, comfort, and compassion mutually shared on a physical, spiritual, and emotional level that encompasses the whole being. Intimacy causes us to slow down to know and experience our spouse more profoundly. It is the ability to connect on a level where you peer into your spouse's soul. *INTIMACY (Innermost Need Tenderly Initiates My Affection Craving You)* goes beyond the flesh and experiences the essence of who they are. It is a deep bond of knowing just who your spouse is. Intimacy means having a good vision for your spouse and what they mean to you.

There are five types of intimacy we need to grow in. Physical intimacy deals with how we touch and caress our spouse to increase their desire for us. Emotional intimacy causes us to open our hearts to love and truly appreciate them. Intellectual intimacy is the meeting of our minds that can see beyond conflicts and respect each other's thoughts and opinions. Sexual intimacy allows for experiences that don't just gratify; they *SATISFY (Satiating A Temptation Is Score For You)*. Spiritual intimacy brings relationships to a higher place of faith and purpose. Increasing physical touch, sharing emotions, communicating, finding purpose together, and making sex a priority will grow your marital intimacy. You don't even know your spouse until you see into them. Grow your intimacy and In-To-Me-See.

1 Corinthians 7:3 Let the husband give his wife the affection owed her, and likewise also the wife her husband.

Better Together

People get married because it is rewarding. We each had dreams and expectations of the rewards of a healthy family, well-adjusted children, emotional support, financial stability, and the joy of having someone to grow **OLD (Our Last Days)** with. I wish I could say it's as easy as 123 and ABC, but it's not that marriage is work. It is learning to operate on a different level with someone you agree with and disagree with simultaneously. Marriage causes you to learn your spouse's preferences, habits, and tempers and navigate around them as they seek to do the same. Sometimes, your spouse will rub you the wrong way, like sandpaper. Only to discover rough edges disappear as we adjust our attitude.

Everything in life takes work from someone. Things that are **EASY (Effortless Application Simplifies Year)** to come by are easy to lose. We must cultivate our marriage to make it good. You have to forgive, forget, and remain loyal. Most of us don't like housework, but we like keeping our homes clean. Marriage work is much the same. We have to do the work first before we can enjoy the benefits. It's not all sunshine, but if you stand under the same umbrella, you can make it through the storm without getting too wet. If you want the rewards, you must put in the necessary work. Be successfully married, and don't be afraid to work at it.

1 Corinthians 7:28 But if you marry, you have not sinned. If a virgin marries, she has not sinned. Yet such will have oppression in the flesh, and I want to spare you.

Time After Time

Younger people who raise families and those with highly competitive jobs often struggle to find time alone. Typically, that tapers off as we grow older and don't feel we need to be in a **RUSH (Racing Urge Says Help)** anymore. We are established in our choices and make the best of our careers without jockeying for positions. The children grow and move out, giving couples more time together. The greatest thing you can give your spouse is your time. Nothing can substitute for it. They marry a person, which is what they want: the person. You must make it quality time if you can't find enough time.

Quality time is about making your time together more meaningful and rewarding. **QUALITY (Quietly Unleashing A Life I Totally Yearn)** represents the depth of your connection and the attention and intentions you have that make each other feel important. When time is short, we must set aside time to give our spouses what they have longed for. This can come in deep conversation, attentiveness, affection, or just doing things you both desire. Whether you are cooking, hiking, or dating, the time spent is to fill your spouse with joy so they remain appreciative and don't feel isolated by you. Quality time is therapy for your marriage; the couch you need will be where you hold hands, knowing they are with you, and you will miss out on nothing.

Colossians 4:5 Walk in wisdom toward those who are outside, redeeming the time.

Being With You

In a world where many couples have to work all day, come home, and spend hours helping with homework, cooking, or working a side business before rolling into bed exhausted, sex takes a back seat. Saying to themselves that they will make love tomorrow repeatedly frustrates a relationship. Maintenance sex refers to regularly scheduled encounters to foster a healthy relationship. Make a **LOVE PLAN (Letting Our Values Emerge Prepared Lovemaking Allows Nurturing)**. You may think that scheduled sex is not fun or romantic, but studies show that over 98% of couples who do it are sexually satisfied. Scheduled sex happens during affairs. This way, you prevent extramarital affairs by having an affair with your spouse.

Make plans to make love. You can think of it less like scheduling and more like thinking ahead. If you're already having regular spontaneous sex, that's great, but most couples are not. Place a sex **CODE (Cipher Others Don't Employ)** on your calendar so only you know what it means. Lean into it with anticipation and place a little fantasy in the mix. Pick up new lingerie and add sexting by texting your spouse a sex appointment that includes a mystery about trying something new. Sometimes, you need to schedule time to be intimate without sex. The purpose is to schedule things that bring you closer together. So, get together and have fun.

1 Corinthians 7:5 Don't deprive one another, unless it is by consent for a season, that you may give yourselves to fasting and prayer, and may be together again, that Satan doesn't tempt you because of your lack of self-control.

We Need To Talk

Have you been approached with the words, "We need to talk?" That's the occasion you need to actively listen most carefully. These are times when we carefully try to choose our words while hoping our spouse is receptive to them. They want to avoid misunderstandings and need our **HEARTS (Hearing Ears Always Respond To Sensitivity)** to focus on what they say. No matter the topic, the underlying cause is disappointment, pain, worry, or concern. Even when calm, they charge each word with emotion but try to reach an agreement and not get into an argument. At this time, we must be actively listening to them more than usual. Sometimes, people say, "I'm fine," when they don't want to discuss what's bothering them. You may have to listen while pulling out what is causing their pain.

The difference between hearing and listening is paying attention. We often hear intending to reply rather than listening to understand. **ACTIVE (A Challenge To Increase Vital Energy)** listening requires you to resist responding, not interrupt, and focus on the words and feelings they express. Seek their thoughts and feelings about your home, children, people, and life. Give them the time to clarify themselves and give well-thought-out responses that look to repair the situation and not defend yourself. It doesn't mean they are correct, but they are hurting and need your sensitivity and support. Let them **TALK (Transfer Allows Listening Kindly)**. Listening to their heart causes their heart to heal. So, switch off bias and defense and listen compassionately.

*Proverbs 19:20 Listen to counsel and receive instruction,
that you may be wise in your latter end.*

Stay Connected

Have you ever felt that your spouse just wasn't with you? Loneliness isn't about who you are around but who you connect to. People can be in a room full of people and feel isolated because no one is engaging to the degree they feel a connection. If everyone else ignores you but you have that one person that you connect to, **LONELY (Living Outcast Needing Emotional Love Yearns)** feelings disappear. There is a reason why most spouses stay together at events. You must ensure your spouse doesn't feel alone in a crowded room or party. If you're the outgoing one, stay by their side until they engage others, then you are free to roam.

Sometimes, we **SUFFER (Sorrow Usually Forces Feeling Endless Regret)** through things alone because we don't want to hinder or burden our spouses. Trying to protect your spouse from the truth of what happened or is happening leads to regret and is a burden too heavy to carry. It's difficult for some to hear, but being lonely is often a decision not to reach out. Connected people create the future. Strengthen your marriage connection by being honest and working together. As the saying goes, "Teamwork makes the dream work." Sharing time, concerns, and yourself will help make your marriage healthy and strong. Ensure you share how you feel and what you are going through with your spouse. You are not alone, so don't isolate but connect with those who care.

Matthew 19:6 So that they are no more two, but one flesh.
What therefore God has joined together, don't let man tear apart.

Let's Get Married

Some are reading this book looking to get married, and this one is for you. First, you should know that there are apps that will help you plan your wedding and form a budget you can agree on. A wedding isn't something you have to go into debt to have. If you haven't saved up, you don't have to spend much money to have a lovely wedding. That's right; you don't have to go without your dream **WEDDING (Wife Earns Day Drawing In New Groom)** because there isn't enough money. Play it smart and ask reliable loved ones to provide services instead of wedding gifts. Spend your money on your rings and honeymoon, and let others supply what you need. You will need about eight dependable people between the two of you.

You can have two people **SPLIT (Separate Parts Left In Tandem)** the reception hall's cost, allowing you to bring in your food. Have one person pay for all the dining wear, another makes your centerpieces, and a final person will pay for the DJ. These are all done weeks in advance, so you won't have problems. If you have three dependable family members who are excellent cooks, have one provide the entree and two others make all the side dishes. If you know someone who bakes and does basic decoration, they can make a cake for you. I have seen weddings where couples pay around $200, and five other people pay for the suit, dress, and everything for the reception. Use what you got when you don't have a lot.

Proverbs 8:14 Counsel and sound knowledge are mine.
I have understanding and power.

We Are The World

Sometimes, we lose someone close, affecting our family deeply. Sometimes, it is someone your spouse grew up knowing, and you aren't as close to them. They take it hard, and you must support them. Other times, it's someone close to you both, and you and your spouse may take turns trying to be strong for each other while grieving. In difficult times, there is no one correct answer you can give, but there is power in your presence while you do what you can to provide comfort and solace. **SOLACE (Surviving Our Loss And Continuing Everyday)** derives itself from the peace of the soul. There are so many trials in the world that you can't fix, but what you can do is help.

Your spouse needs you to help them find the center of their peace and help them navigate through the seven stages of grief (shock, denial, anger, bargaining, sadness, acceptance, processing). Helping your spouse find solace requires us to provide a peaceful environment through comforting and kind words that can open them to a new perspective. Please think of the first five stages as things out of our control, and the last two stages of **GRIEF (Growing Regret Inpacts Everyday Feelings)** are under your control. Provide your spouse **SOLACE (Support Of Loving Attitude Comforts Everyone)** to help until they reach the acceptance stage and begin processing their healing.

2 Corinthians 1:4 who comforts us in all our affliction, that we may be able to comfort those who are in any affliction, through the comfort with which we ourselves are comforted by God.

Be Still

In this fast-paced, busy world, we need to take the time to slow things down a little. We receive so many instructions, information, and issues that our minds are flooded and overloaded. Take it **SLOW (Stop Letting Others Win)** so confusion doesn't cause you to miss anything important or lose an opportunity. Slowing down allows us to comprehend conversations, appreciate actions, and find solutions. Our world is fast-paced enough, so your relationship doesn't have to. Take your time with each other when you talk. Take time to look at what's going on and take time to handle your issues. Better planning leads to better results.

Slowing down is sometimes the best way to reset and speed up. Though you may always be **BUSY (Buried Under Someone's Yoke)**, you don't have to do anything with a rushed spirit. Slowing down takes patience. Patience is the virtue we need the most when we mess up and want a chance to fix and get them right. Patience is also what we like the least when we are in need. **SLOW (Steps Leisurely Ordered Win)** down to ensure you focus on the most important things. We live one moment at a time, so make sure they count. Slowing down ensures we enjoy, examine, and appreciate the good things we have in life, including our spouse. It's a precious gift to give our families what they need most. That's why we slow down to smell the roses.

Lamentations 3:25 Yahweh is good to those who wait for him,
to the soul who seeks him.

Endless Love

You may have married someone who has a lot of good qualities, but they aren't an affectionate person. Some grew up lacking parental or guardians affection. They learned to operate through their affection deprivation, where love is understood as present but not discussed. The deficit leads to internal struggles to show *AFFECTION (A Fond Feeling Expressing Care That Involves Our Needs)*, which takes time to heal. Not being affectionate may work for a while when we are so busy that we are distracted, but eventually, at least one of you may feel they are missing something. It's good to come out of your shell and the hustle and bustle of life to kiss, hug, and acknowledge your spouse daily.

Think of affection as a shortened version of the Affect-I'm-On. It may be your way of operating but not your spouse's. People can know they are loved without feeling valued. Affection deprivations cause a fragile heart through doubt and a fear of rejection while creating a need for security and attention. If you suffer from an affection deficit, you must practice self-care, communicate your needs, and seek your spouse's support. If you are unaffectionate, *ENSURE (Establish New Standard Using Revitalized Encouragement)* you never let someone be more attentive to your spouse's needs than you. If they are, your spouse's desire will drift from you to the object that fulfills their need from the deficit you have caused.

Romans 12:10 In love of the brothers be tenderly
affectionate to one another;
in honor prefer one another.

Seventy Times 7

Everyone gets angry, but not everyone deals with anger problems. Anger affects our decision-making and often manifests through our verbal expressions and physical aggressions. Anger derives typically from an offense or injury to one's sense of pride. Yes, anger is pride in disguise. To deal with your *ANGER (Allowing Negativity Gets Enlarged Resentment)*, you must address the sources of your pride and frustrations. Seeing a wrong produces righteous anger, giving us the energy to fix a problem. Feeling wronged produces harmful anger that, when misdirected, harms our family. There are anger management classes everywhere; the only court order you need is the appeal to wholeness in your family.

Under no circumstances is *ABUSE (A Behavior Using Sinful Exploits)* tolerable. Anger doesn't need a reason to lose control. If you ever put your hands on your spouse, don't wait to see if it will happen again. Seek serious counseling. You are to speak to your spouse, not hit them. If your spouse deals with harmful anger, you must be assertive and set boundaries. Choose your battles wisely and meet their frustration with peace. Don't let their anger become yours. Anger often covers up other emotions, so remain compassionate and forgiving but never tolerate abuse. Foster peace and work towards resolving anger before it becomes a problem.

Matthew 18:21-22 Then Peter came and said to him, "Lord, how often shall my brother sin against me, and I forgive him? Until seven times?" Jesus said to him, "I don't tell you until seven times, but, until seventy times seven.

Treat Them Like They Want To Be Treated

Make sure others don't feel what makes you feel bad. That's one variation of the Golden Rule, or should we say **RULES (Restrictions Utilizing Limits Engaging Standards)**, as it shows up in multiple religions and philosophies around the globe. The **GOLDEN RULE (Giving Out Love Daily Eases Negative Responses Using Little Empathy)** works when we empathize and imagine how we would feel if we were in someone else's shoes and treat them as we would want to be. In marriage, this means showing kindness, thoughtfulness, respect, and building each other. It means taking an empathy-first approach when addressing your spouse or children, starting conversations favorably, and making connections before corrections.

We are to give what we want to receive. Suppose you **GIVE (Generous Individuals Voluntarily Enlisted)** your spouse anger, grief, or frustration. They will receive it, multiply what you gave, and return it to you. In there lies the heart of many of our problems. Too often, we get what we have created. The Golden Rule is an ethic of reciprocity. It has boundaries to prevent misuse. Many have committed the Golden Rule to memory but not to life. If you give love, comfort, and understanding, you should expect to receive it back eventually. If it's not occurring, then use considerate conversation to discover why. But always seek to be what you want to receive and make your marriage golden.

Luke 6:31 As you would like people to do to you, do exactly so to them.

I Can See Clearly Now

No matter how long it took, we won the hand of our spouse, and now we are married. Many tend to put a lot of energy into the courting process and begin wavering during the relationship. Through sharing our future hopes, dreams, and ideas, we introduce a version of ourselves that our future spouse expects to see one day. Our job is to become the man or woman they envision we can be. That person is in you, and often, your spouse will encourage you to become that better **VISION (Valuable Ideas Support Insights Of Needs)** they see, but you no longer accept. Whether it was time, difficulty, or accepting that your former thoughts weren't for you, your spouse expects you to become someone meaningful in character and life.

The dreams we have tossed aside remain alive in them, and though they accept they may have changed, they still expect them to become something relevant. Like wine, **ACCEPT (Allowing Conditions Can Earn Personal Triumph)** that you will improve with time. Yet wine doesn't just sit in a barrel. Fermentation converts the energy in the grape, transforming it into something new. Your spouse doesn't expect you to sit there but to take the energy in you and become what they see. Your spouse sees your potential, so accept the vision they promote through compliments, corrections, and charges for you to implement and improve.

John 2:10 and said, "Everyone serves the fine wine first,
and then the cheap wine after the guests are drunk.
But you have saved the fine wine until now!"

Celluloid Heroes

Has your spouse ever called you when they know you're unavailable? It happens when they are troubled, lonely, or bored and need to hear your **VOICE** *(Vocalizing Our Internal Cares Effectively)* to encourage and elevate their mood. They can feel slightly disappointed when they can't reach you, and a computerized voicemail doesn't help. Every couple should have a text code to differentiate between a typical call and a call that needs to interrupt everything. Sometimes, they want to hear you. But for non-emergencies, you need a way for them to reach you without reaching you.

Start a personal interest channel on YouTube or another social media outlet that lets you keep content private for your spouse. Post videos with special **LEAD *(Love, Encouragement, Appreciation, Dedication)*** messages for your spouse. They can watch it when they miss you while you are away. Post them on Facebook, and have the kids post videos on your spouse's **CHANNEL *(Carrier Hosting A Network Needs Established Location)***. Even if you only post one video a month, 20 years from now, you will have hundreds of videos that chronicle your thoughts and how you age together. Your channel will ensure that wherever you may be, you will always be in their heart. If tragedy ever strikes, your family will have all the love, encouragement, and advice you left behind on the channel made just for them.

Matthew 26:11 For you always have the poor with you,
but you don't always have me.

There You'll Be

A significant key to success is to become an influencer. Famous and successful people influence others in business, politics, religion, or social media. An influencer is someone who affects decisions. You don't just need good influences; you need constant ones. Adults and children are usually attracted to the most impactful and consistent influences around them. An occasional good **INFLUENCE (Integrity Nourishes Faith Letting Us Encourage Nurtured Connections Effectively)** usually isn't enough to redirect character. However, constantly staying in good company with those achieving goals and having good marriages causes us to desire to reach for our potential.

A mirror **REFLECTS (Reproducing Emulates Features Lasting Effects Causing Temporary Simulation)** our faces, but what we are like is reflected in the faces of the company we keep. When you're around good influences, you will become a good influencer. You never know who is watching you, but someone always is. We become examples as our interactions communicate our integrity, intentions, and interests to others. Yet sometimes, we are instead setting bad examples by not walking in our best selves. All of us mess up, but it's what we have consistently been that will leave an impact on our loved ones. Live consciously of the type of influencers you have and are, and leave an imprint on your marriage and family.

1 Corinthians 15:33 Don't be deceived! "Evil companionships corrupt good morals."

Frustrated

Don't frustrate yourself. Frustration happens when we are blocked from achieving our desires and designs or satisfying instinctive drives and remain too inflexible to adjust. External frustrations impede progress, but our internal frustrations impede us. Frustration can cause us to think negatively about our lives and spouses. Internal frustrations often cause us to look at our spouses as if they are the cause, even when they have no control over the wants, needs, and demands we have. Frustration can lead to anger arousal, withdrawal, and compulsive behavior, which we must deal with. Likely, our spouse has a solution we can't see. Still, we can't receive solutions from what we see as a **SOURCE *(Someone Originated Useful Resources Causing Events)*** of our problems.

Frustrations deal with our unmet expectations, so we are the only ones who can handle them. We must **FRUSTRATE *(Fighting Rash Uncontrolled Situations Though Rough Around The Edges)*** our frustration by blocking the thoughts that block us. Giving up on frustrations doesn't mean you must give up your goals, but you may have to adjust your timetable. Some have learned to turn their frustrations into dedication, inspiration, or fascination. Things that you can't change, you must accept them as they are and move on. What you can change most is you, so put frustrations aside and deal with the issues honestly and openly.

John 16:33 I have told you these things, that in me you may have peace. In the world you have trouble; but cheer up! I have overcome the world.

Losing My Religion

Your spouse could be great, but that doesn't mean you won't lose your desire for them. There are two types of desires; both include emotions but are different and can change like them. *DESIRE (Deep Emotions Suggest I'm Really Eager)* either rises, leading to emotion, or derives from the emotion itself. Desires arise from thoughts such as the need for financial security, which can make you emotional about getting a specific job. Other desires come from emotions, like desiring to sleep with someone you love. Typically, losing desire for a spouse means new thoughts have overridden or overwhelmed the desires that rise out of emotion.

Losing desire is similar to losing your *PATH (People Attempting To Help)*. You must return to the right road, discover what you hold against your spouse, and heal it. Usually, that will allow it to return slowly. Also, have yourself checked out to see if there is a hormonal imbalance or a medical issue. If those don't work, revisit what attracted you to them in the first place. If it's not there, find something new that is good about them, then compliment them on the things you like so they will do them more often. Without desire, we have no motivation, causing your marriage to fill up with rifts, rejection, and retaliation. Clear your mind of can't. Fix your heart by finding your desire and keeping good things in your thoughts.

Proverbs 13:12 Hope deferred makes the heart sick,
but when longing is fulfilled, it is a tree of life.

My Head & My Heart

Married life has ups and downs, mountains, valleys, and everything in between. Tough times require tough decisions. Though we don't want to miss opportunities, we don't want to make a big mistake through sudden decisions. When we have hard choices, the first decision we should make is not to be rushed. People tend to want answers immediately. It would help to base decisions on your priorities, not someone else's urgency. Having a sense of urgency doesn't mean you shouldn't take some time to reflect. Give yourself time to **DECIDE (Data Effectively Considered Is Duly Engaged)**. Rushed decisions can hurt or cause drastic life changes.

Our values come from our hearts and our reasoning from our heads, so we need them to work together. Many people go along to get along, following decisions others make for them. When others make your decisions, you follow their priorities, not yours. No one outside of your marriage should be making decisions for you. The more you practice making decisions that you stand by, the easier it becomes. Think about the decision and write down your options. **CHOOSE (Choices Hear Other Options Supporting Efforts)** options that align with your values and priorities and cast away any fear you may have. The best decision is yours, so do what's best for your family. Stand by it, even when it's hard or unpopular. The choice is yours.

Isaiah 30:21 and when you turn to the right hand, and when you turn to the left, your ears will hear a voice behind you, saying, "This is the way. Walk in it."

Happy Together

Successful people *LEARN (Listening Educates A Reasoning Novice)* to work well with others and harness their talents and hard skills. Hard skills are technical skills learned through education and training that make them valuable to a business. Soft skills are the habits and traits we use to work with others, such as communication skills, cooperation, collaboration, and conflict resolution. As a spouse, marriage is your business. You may not feel successful, but you can work successfully with your spouse. Working alongside your spouse brings your home into order and makes you more than you ever could be alone. Working with a shared vision and goals can make the impossible possible.

Don't let your spouse do all of anything. If they are constantly the ones everyone depends on for cleaning, washing, and taking off work when the kids are sick, they may feel you are not supportive of them. Incredible things happen when you support each other. Your *SUPPORT (Service Unleashing Preferred Progress Often Requires Toughness)* means every-thing to your spouse, so make everything a "We Thing." Your decisions are now jointly made, so consider new input and try a new way of doing things to discover if you have the best model. Whether it's house chores, business ideas, or recreational activities, work together to simplify things. Alone, you can do little; together, you can accomplish much.

Hebrews 10:24 Let's consider how to provoke one another
to love and good works,

Moving Forward

There are too many marriages where one or more partner has unresolved feelings from their past. Unresolved feelings deal with emotions we have tried to repress rather than resolve. Because they are left unattended, they become emotional traps and time bombs carried within us that can spring up unintentionally. It's hard to move forward if things are weighing you down. It would be best if you denounced previous relationships, soul ties, hurts, and traumatic events to separate you from them. Letting go is not always easy, but it is necessary. If hurt, review the events and recognize that certain things were not your fault. If you did the hurting, look back on your mistakes, accept them as a thing of the *PAST (Preoccupation About Sad Times)*, and dedicate yourself to moving towards the future.

Our past is a stepping stone, so don't use it as a millstone holding you back. We can't change what happened, but we can learn to resolve emotions and separate them from memories so we don't relive them. Don't get worn down by things you should have conquered long ago. Every relationship you had before the current one failed. If it didn't, you would still be in it. Look at your marriage as your first chance to get it right. Thoughts of old failures *STEAL (Stripping Their Effectiveness Allows Looting)* your future. Guarantee your future by leaving the past behind.

Philippians 3:13 Brothers, I don't regard myself as yet having taken hold, but one thing I do: forgetting the things which are behind and stretching forward to the things which are before,

Every Day

To appreciate means to add worth to someone or something. Whether self-satisfaction or public recognition, everyone wants appreciation for their good deeds. Never take for granted that what your spouse does is just their **DUTY (Deeds Undertaken To Yourself)**. They voluntarily serve you, and it should be recognized. You are a mirror for the brightness of those around you. Acknowledge their worth and let them shine. To acknowledge is to acclaim knowledge. A few words here and there daily add value to your spouse and show them how much more they are worth. You are just showing them that you know what they do, and they know what they mean to you. They will work harder and be happier when acknowledged.

Showing appreciation and acknowledgment improves our spouse's mood and sets a good atmosphere for our homes. There are several ways to **ACKNOWLEDGE (Admitting Conscious Knowledge Needs Our Words Lets Every Deed Get Encouraged)** your spouse. You can never express gratitude too soon, but you can do it too late, so make it a habit of saying thank you when they do something. Our spouse won't see our appreciation unless our gratitude is actionable; look for those times they do extra and give them a small reward such as a big hug, kiss, or a nice meal. Show them you know them by giving them not what you want but what they want, and they will feel acknowledged and appreciated.

1 Thessalonians 5:11 Therefore exhort one another,
and build each other up, even as you also do.

New Rules

Many of us had fairy tale dreams that ours would be the **PERFECT (Positive Effect Reveals Faithfulness Ensures Complete Trust)** marriage. Why not? Your spouse is great, even if it's difficult to remember that now. Some of us are not living happily ever after. Troubles and disagreements may have slipped in. Perhaps you were two good forgivers initially, but grace gaps and forgiveness failures now exist. The best time to fix a problem is before it starts. Now is the best time to start if you haven't done that. When we aren't succeeding in business, athletics, or other endeavors, you don't change the team; you change the **TACTICS (Their Attitude Controls Things Involving Changing Situation).**

You can fix what you're willing to change. Push **RESET (Remember Every Situation Encourages Transformation)** by focusing on strengthening what is still functioning right. Get rid of things that aren't essential, and go back to the bare necessities. We can reset our attitude by reflecting on good qualities when discouraged, upset, or tired. If your communication and ways of operating aren't working, try a new strategy, forgive more, and allow your partner to take over things you failed at. Attend seminars, couples' groups, or therapy to get fresh ideas and work on gaining a new perspective. You can have a new marriage with the same spouse, so push the reset button before your marriage falls apart.

1 Peter 5:10 But may the God of all grace, who called you to his eternal glory by Christ Jesus, after you have suffered a little while, perfect, establish, strengthen, and settle you.

Nothing Is Lost

How do you *REPAIR (Restoration Ensures Progress As I'm Reconstructed)* things when you have messed up big time? Eventually, saying sorry wears out its welcome because your spouse doesn't care what you say if you don't change. Once you plant a seed, it grows, and the longer it takes to rectify it, the more effort you will take to uproot. However, uprooting the problem leaves a gap that needs something new planted to fill it in. You may have to encourage your spouse and express love on eight occasions to uproot the damage after apologizing for one harmful word spoken that grew in their heart. Damaging actions may require you to restrict some things that remove your focus at least temporarily and cut other things off permanently.

You may not like to spend a lot, but regret gifts open doors to atonement. Regret gifts are expressions of remorse in *GIFT (Giving Increases Faithful Trust)* form to help atone for a wrong done. These gifts are not to show appreciation but to acknowledge the wrongdoing that you are committing to work on. A flurry of small gifts or kindnesses daily or weekly, as mentioned in tip #4, is better to foster a regular sense of appreciation. Like an *APOLOGY (Acknowledging Prior Offense Lets Out Genuine You)*, repeated regret gifts will lose their potency if a behavior change doesn't accompany them. Regret gifts similar to make-up sex shouldn't cover wrong but let you get past it so you can work it out.

Proverbs 21:14 A gift in secret pacifies anger,
and a bribe in the cloak, strong wrath.

With A Little Help From My Friends

When people bring you their problems, it isn't a bad thing. At least in their minds, it says that you have things together. But keep it together by not letting others inundate you with too many problems. Offer the help, but not at the expense of your family. If you're missing your kid's game because someone needed to speak to you badly about their marital problems and how their spouse says they aren't attentive, then you just repeated their mistake by ignoring your children. Most **ISSUES (Intimate Situations Should Use Ernest Support)** are pressing issues and not urgent. People call with urgency because they are emotional about problems they have allowed to fester for so long that they explode. If you don't want to be in the same boat, give your house the time and attention it needs.

Everyone has some **PROBLEM (People Robbing Our Blessing Leave Everything Messy)** that needs fixing. Take care not to allow emotional appeals to cause you to make mistakes. Don't lend what you can't lose because many people in financial need often don't handle their responsibilities well. Make sure you know who you are dealing with because people with bad character will put you in vulnerable positions to promote what they want. When people have problems, remember to make your family the priority. Help only one person at a time, and always help the ones nearest you, including your family.

Proverbs 3:27 Don't withhold good from those to whom it is due, when it is in the power of your hand to do it.

The Greatest Love Of All

Everyone needs love and acceptance. It's the core of who we are as social beings. There is an entire movement in society encouraging us to love and accept those different from us. I hope you never have to go through what some endure having a child who is different because of some genetic problem or accident that left them with disabilities or deformations. If you do, you have some of us on your side. It's tough, but you will make it. Being immature, children may act cruelly in these situations, be that parent who teaches them otherwise. However, leadership and instruction start at the top. First, you must deal with your **PREJUDICES (Problems Regarding Each Judgment Used Discriminately Involving Chauvinisms Enmity Selection)** and harmful thoughts, even about not accepting your spouse for who they are.

One of the greatest gifts you can ever give your spouse is simply letting them be who they are. Don't try to change them, treating them as if they are a hindrance or problem. Love and accept them for who they are; they will feel valued. You don't have to love their flaws, but love them despite them. Show them their **VALUE (Vision And Leadership Unites Everyone)** by accepting, acknowledging, and encouraging them. It takes great love to overlook flaws and see value. Once they accept their value regardless of their flaws, no one can use their flaws against them. Helping them do that is one of the greatest loves you can give.

*Romans 15:7 Therefore accept one another,
even as Christ also accepted you, to the glory of God.*

Hold My Hand

Decide to love again. Unselfish love can only come from a decision to love unconditionally. Let's unpack the Agape/Altruistic love from tip #121. Some call this a self-sacrificing, unselfish love. The highest point of love is the decision to love someone regardless of how it makes us feel. It means loving your spouse through whatever life throws at you. There is something to say about **LOVE (Loyalty Overcoming Vice Effectively)**, never giving up. It is not only the love that chooses you but chooses you over and over again as you grow together. This love doesn't advocate being abused because it has standards. However, it does mean that when the offender wants to turn things around, we will support change when it is genuine.

We think of ourselves when we say we don't love our spouse. Real love does not focus on **SELF (Stingy Emotions Lose Favor)** but on others. You can love your spouse in one thousand different ways if you set your mind to love without conditions or restraint. Think about the times when you wanted to be loved unconditionally. Often, we reserve this type of love for our children and grandchildren, but spreading a little of it for our spouse also goes a long way. If we tell ourselves that we no longer love our spouse, our heart will eventually get the **MESSAGE (Memo Ensuring Subject Spoken Always Gains Ear)**. So, hold on to your love and keep giving love, speaking it to your heart till you can't give it anymore.

1 Corinthians 13:7 bears all things, believes all things,
hopes all things, and endures all things.

I Can't Get No Satisfaction

We know how to love our spouse, but there are things that they need that may be hidden. Complaining is a form of communication that relays discontent and dissatisfaction. Complaints reveal the mysteries of what is happening in our spouse's heart. We get distracted with the delivery and miss the message. Please don't get mad at complaints, but listen to them. When they **COMPLAIN (Creation Of More Problems Lets Accusations Increase Negativity)**, they are explaining why they are unsettled, unsatisfied, and what is unacceptable. We complain about what is most important to us or what is lacking. You may feel your giving love, but not all of us receive love the same way. If your spouse complains, it may be because you might give them the wrong attention, action, or attitude.

Complaining and **VENTING (Voicing Emotional Needs To Improve Normal Good)** are similar, but venting is about letting emotions go. Complaining focuses and holds onto negatives. No one enjoys it if you're the one who complains a lot. Complaints are not needed to relieve stress or strategically get your point across. Constant complaining creates a victim mentality that seeks validation. Complaints should be rare and instrumental in fixing problems. Spouses want your heart's mystery, not your muttering mouth. Learn how to reframe situations and put a bit of gratitude for the good things. Be wise and complain well.

Psalm 55:2 Attend to me, and answer me.
I am restless in my complaint, and moan

Late Night Talking

The wealthy name their homes to give added significance to them. Likewise, some of us named our very first car because it was important to us. What name do you call your spouse? It should be sweet and relevant to them. Call them by that name and not out of their name. Titles show ownership, responsibility, and honor, so give them a title that builds them up and stick with it. No matter how mad you get, they are still your spouse, and you should never replace a respectful **TITLE *(Term Identifying The Labeled Epithet)*** with a profane name. Calling your spouse something you should never let others call them is unacceptable and shows a lack of support.

The prefix "Dis" means not or against, so when we say disadvantage, we mean no advantage, dislike, not liking, disorder, no order. To discuss would, therefore, relate to us not cussing. People cuss to joke around, release anger, or show enthusiasm. It may help you, but it doesn't help the conversation. Some people cuss so much that if they put $5 in the cuss jar every time, they did it, they would have money for a vacation. We need to have conversations so that no matter how upset we get, we don't use words of disrespect or disregard. Learn to **DISCUSS *(Dialogue I Should Create Understands Spouses Stance)*** things and not rant about them. Arguments find problems, discussions find solutions. So, learn to discuss and stop the cussing.

Ephesians 4:29 Let no corrupt speech proceed out of your mouth, but only what is good for building others up as the need may be, that it may give grace to those who hear.

Secrets

How secure are you in your marriage? Let's form a little test: "Does your spouse know all your secrets, or are you holding back?" While some truths may be left unsaid, serious matters must never become secrets, even when they hurt. Secrets are measurements of your relationship's security and commitment. The things we **HIDE (Haunted Intimidation Disguises Experiences)** reveal fear, dishonesty, and a lack of trust. We deceive ourselves, saying they could never handle it if they knew. Some feel justified with secrets, fearing they could affect their relationship, disappoint, or hurt their spouse. Spouses are more resilient than we give them credit for. The more you expose yourself to your spouse, the more secure you and your spouse will be. Your right to privacy ends when it can negatively affect your family.

You may say, "I'm going to take this one to the grave." But things have a way of coming out. Many secrets deal with deceiving your spouse, having them think one thing when the truth is far from it. Often, the lie is worse than the **SECRET (Silently Encouraging Confidentiality Rights Erases Trust)**. Hiding secrets says to your spouse that you don't believe they have your best interest in mind. If your spouse learns what you tried to hide from someone other than you, it could devastate them. Please do not give them lies, half-truths, or deception. We design secrets in a way that causes their discovery with time. Always be upfront, and you will never get left behind.

Luke 8:17 For nothing is hidden that will not be revealed,
nor anything secret that will not be known and come to light.

See A Victory

Motivation is one of the most potent factors in success, happiness, and completing anything. Motivation deals with the reason for your actions. We each have near-limitless potential, but what separates us is opportunity, preparation, and motivation. Motivation can be intrinsic, dealing with what drives you, or extrinsic, in seeking your goals. There is a motivation for all our actions and an un-motivator for our inaction. It's never too late to become what you want to be, but you won't go far unless you have something *MOTIVATE (Moving Others To Initiate Victorious Actions Takes Encouragement)* you. Some un-motivators for inaction in marriage are inconsideration, apathy, self-centeredness, bitterness, and frustration.

If you are not acting upon your responsibilities or your spouse's needs or desires, you may have one of these un-motivators working on you. It is easier to set goals than build what drives you, so define your career and character development goals. Next, achieve a few small goals to build momentum and motivation. Give yourself a small reward for your achievements to build a positive attitude. Grant time for the big things, accept setbacks, and be grateful. If your spouse *LACKS (Losing Attitude Consistently Kills Strengths)* motivation, reinforce the small things they do and they will desire to do more. Remember, what doesn't challenge you doesn't change you. Press forward in the small steps, and you will see big rewards.

Romans 12:11 not lagging in diligence, fervent in spirit, serving the Lord.

They Reminisce Over You (T.R.O.Y)

We started by carving our names on trees, moved to tattoos, and now, we have license plates stating our love. These are declarations to the world and reminders of our love. The ring is another way to **REMIND (Refreshing Encourages My Increasing Natural Desires)** us. We have several rings we may receive. A class ring tells every one of your achievements and steps toward maturity. A mood ring shows how we feel at a given time and helps us see where to improve. A promise ring certifies our commitment to each other and that we will stick together through the tough times. The engagement ring declares our intentions and that we will fully engage in our relationship and act to make it permanent.

The wedding **RING (Round Instrument Nurtures Growth)** symbolizes all four. It declares our love, commitment, and graduation to a new relationship, which we must actively engage to maintain. Ring reminders are the habit of looking at your ring and affirming your commitment during troubles and temptations. Don't fall for the temptation to hide or remove your ring when speaking to someone you find attractive. Look at your ring and silently recite a portion of your vows. Let your ring remind you to mention your spouse when you have an extended conversation with someone from the opposite sex. Engrave your commitment in your mind, tattoo it in your heart, and let the world know your license to succeed.

2 Peter 1:12 Therefore I will not be negligent to remind you of these things, though you know them and are established in the present truth.

Thank You

Having manners is not about saying "Thank you, or You're welcome." It's about all forms of recognition and decent behavior. Learning etiquette can save embarrassment at social gatherings. When the occasion arises, people want their spouse to have a little **CLASS (Conducts Life As Socially Sophisticated)**. Some people believe it's all about dining rules, but businesses wouldn't teach it if that were so. Etiquette involves social graces that maximize our contacts. It includes the best way to introduce yourself, have considerate conversations, listen, and make people comfortable. A significant thing that most don't consider about etiquette is that the most considerable portion is developing social skills and character building.

If etiquette seemed restraining, I would like you to consider taking a second look. Just as if your spouse loved to dance and you're no good at it, you can easily take a class; etiquette is the same. If there are no classes in your area, watch YouTube videos and practice what you learned on your next date. Good **MANNERS (Methods Acquired Nurture Needed Etiquette Require Study)** lead to great conversations. Good manners reflect respect for yourself and consideration for others. Manners will take you where education and entitlement cannot. Plus, you have the bonus of making great outings with your spouse.

Proverbs 17:27-28 He who spares his words has knowledge. He who is even tempered is a man of understanding. Even a fool, when he keeps silent, is counted wise. When he shuts his lips, he is thought to be discerning.

Stressed Out

There are many reasons why someone may become insecure in a relationship. Some may be **INSECURE (I Need Safe Effective Control Used Regularly Everyday)** due to past actions or inactions by their spouse, such as lack of intimacy, distraction, or forgetting important events. These can make a usually confident person wonder a bit. However, people who attach their identity and value to the time others invest in them will become insecure. Insecurity deals with things we want control of but are out of our hands. The issue is that insecurities **SABOTAGES (Systematic Action Bringing Obstacles To Achieving Goals Endures Struggling)** relationships.

Insecurity works like a self-fulfilling prophecy because fear of losing someone causes us to be defensive and drive them away. People who look for something wrong will find or **INVENT (If Not Validated, Enlist Novel Thoughts)** it in their minds. They tend to project insecurities onto others as problems or flaws in them. Sometimes, we are insecure because we know our spouse deserves more than we give. Often, insecure people dislike others when there is no good reason. Holding onto past insecurities, anger, and jealousies brings bondage into relationships. It all starts with a decision. Ridding ourselves of insecurity requires identifying triggers, reaffirming our confidence, and communicating properly. When an insecure idea arises, get rid of it before it gets rid of what you do have.

1 John 4:18 There is no fear in love; but perfect love casts out fear, because fear has punishment. He who fears is not made perfect in love.

Love Is A Battlefield

Our link between behavior and emotion runs both ways. The Stanford prison experiment proved that the fastest way to change emotions is to change their associated behaviors. Our emotions affect our actions, but our actions affect our emotions similarly. Have you noticed how pretend couples start liking each other? Your heart will eventually **MIRROR (Modulated Image Readers Reflection Of Representation)** your behavior. There are links to things like inactivity and increased depression and how acting in love can cause you to fall in love. Changing behavior will increase or decrease social interactions that will positively or negatively affect how you feel, depending on the changes made.

If you lack empathy, interest, and affection, changing your actions and behaving as someone who has fallen in love can readjust your heart. Your **HEART (Having Encouragement And Respect Together)** will begin to feel how you act and respond by accepting new emotions. Our actions dictate our attitude, and our attitude informs us to think differently so that our hearts change. Whatever acts of love you **PERFORM (Plan Effectively Reviewed For Optimizing Regular Movement)** will cause your heart to conform. Readjust your heart by not giving up on being an attentive, affectionate, and honest communicator; your heart will feel what you do.

Proverbs 16:4 Commit thy works unto the LORD,
and thy thoughts shall be established. (KJV)

Last Time That I Checc'd

Think of your marriage as a bank account into which you deposit valuables. A joint account means you can withdraw anytime; however, you can only withdraw what you deposit. A certificate of deposit (CD) invests over a long time, so you gain their interest. Savings require preparations before problems arise and doing what is needed to meet your goals. Your checking **ACCOUNT (Always Consider Choices Or Use New Tactics)** requires that you check to ensure how your spouse is doing before taking anything out. You also have daily withdrawal limits on your card that you must get permission to exceed so you don't take too much at a time. These five bank accounts involve corporate cooperation (joint), cultivation (CD), choice (savings), consideration (checking), and communication (withdrawal limits).

Trying to withdraw something that's not there leaves your spouse depleted and you in debt to make new deposits. If you haven't deposited love, honor, and truth into your own life, then it won't be possible for your spouse to withdraw. Start by depositing positive thoughts in your mind. Make sure you have the right things in your heart so that the right things will come out in your actions. Take care not to **DEPLETE (Drained Emotions Produce Lower Energy Through Exhaustion)** what you deposit, and your marriage will remain healthy and strong.

Proverbs 31:11 The heart of her husband trusts in her.
He shall have no lack of gain.

Two Lovers

Some believe they can love more than one person at a time; even if this is true, You can't be committed to more than one. **SPLIT (Single Piece Left Is Torn)** love causes emotional dissonance where the expected emotions we display conflict with our true feelings. Emotional dissonance leaves us with an internal struggle that deepens rifts we may already be experiencing with our spouse, leading to a grass greener on the other side mentality where the illusion of another relationship is greater than the allurement of ours. Devotion requires a singular focus. No one should have to convince you that there is no one out there for you except the one you are with.

Never take a two-lover mindset into a marriage because it will become the measuring line of how much you value your relationship. The grass seems greener, but the water bill is too high to cross over. You can lose everything important, and it typically doesn't work out. If you're married but in love with someone else, ask yourself how you let it happen. What is it about them that you find missing in your spouse? **COMMIT (Cultivation Of My Marriage Is Trustworthy)** to your spouse and break off any contact you may have with the other person. If they work with you and you can't change jobs, change your division or hours. Then, work on watering your own grass and see how your marriage springs back to life.

Matthew 8:24 No one can serve two masters, for either he will hate the one and love the other, or else he will be devoted to one and despise the other. You can't serve both God and Mammon.

Unbreak My Heart

If you're wondering if you are the problem in your relationship, the answer is at least partially yes. People tend to play the **VICTIM (Vulnerable Individual Caught Through Injuries Misfortune)**, the strong one, or the savior of the relationship, and consider others the problem. But we know victims are often manipulators, strong people are at times secretly depressed, and those with a savior complex might want recognition. However, those who think they are the problem are likely honest about their behaviors. People can act dysfunctional at times, lashing out and, on rare occasions, even planning to punish their partner in some fashion. If this becomes a **TREND (Times Repeated Endeavors Need Directing)**, you are the hurtful one who needs healing before you can repair the damage.

Once you **BREAK (Behavior Rips Emotions Apart Knowingly)** your spouse's heart, it is difficult to put the pieces back together again. Showing remorse, kindness, and consideration is helpful, but getting help from yourself is also necessary. You cannot fix what you will not face. There is nothing wrong with seeking professional help. We do it when we need things that are too difficult to fix, build, or organize. It's like a guided tour to help you work through your problems while healing the damage that you caused. Fixing your thinking will often fix your problems; then, you can work on returning the pieces to your home.

Psalms 147:3 He heals the broken in heart, and binds up their wounds.

I Belong To You

What does it mean to say something or someone is ours? When your home is yours, it means ownership, but we do not own our children. We have unique relationships with them, including stewardship responsibilities. As long as we hold guardianship for **OUR (Owner Use Restricted)** children, the law can punish us for neglect. They are ours, not as property like a car but as a loan from above. Your spouse belongs to you but not as property, so don't treat them that way. The **ROOT (Resource Offering Our Trouble)** of harmful jealousy treats people as objects of ownership. Your spouse has given their heart to you as a loan and is not to be controlled through domination, manipulation, or intimidation.

Your marriage is not just yours. If it belongs to anyone, it is God's. Please treat each other like a loaner, and you must ensure you return to its maker better off than you received it. There is nothing we have that we cannot lose, so we should treat ownership loosely. Only inanimate things can be property, and we still can't do just anything we want with our land, cars, or homes. We call cats and dogs furry friends to understand they are our property only in the sense of partnership and stewardship responsibility. Every living thing in our life is on **LOAN (Lending Offered Accommodates Need)** to meet our physical, mental, and emotional needs. We are responsible for how we handle ourselves and all we have, including our marriages.

1 Corinthians 6:19 Or don't you know that your body
is a temple of the Holy Spirit who is in you, whom
you have from God? You are not your own,

Jesus At The Centre

Your marriage has three possible centers, and whatever you center it on will be the target that receives the shots. The self-centered marriage is focused on the selfish nature and believes in its greatness. Self-centered means that your spouse is a sacrifice to meet your goals and promote your agenda. They are the target that takes all the shots, but you are the attraction that takes **CENTER (Centrally Exposed Nucleus Transforms Every Result)** and receives all the credit. This isn't as much a marriage as it is a marketplace of one's ego. The children-centered marriage focuses on what's best for our offspring. The parents sacrifice attempting to raise well-balanced children. Since the efforts focus on the children, there is little development as a couple. When kids move, the center is removed, and the marriage falls apart.

The us-centered relationship focuses on the needs of all involved. We take the hits together, lessening the blows, and rejoice in each other's victories as if we all have achieved them together. Consideration, support, and humility are needed to get your marriage out of **HARM's (Having A Risky Moment)** way. When we include God, our us-centered becomes God-with-us-centered, throwing ours and the enemy's focus on Him. God will take the brunt of the attack and become the center of adoration as we rejoice in the good things. Celebrating Him as He celebrates us is the glue keeping us focused and together.

Matthew 11:28 Come to me, all you who labor and are heavily burdened, and I will give you rest.

Satisfaction

Let me start by saying there was nothing wrong with being single. There are millions of happy and well-adjusted singles. However, statistics inform us that married people live longer, **HAVE (Home Allowing Victory Emerges)** higher incomes, own homes more often, have a better support system and are healthier than singles. Being married has many benefits, such as better sleep patterns, improved mental wellness, and an ideal environment for child-rearing. Some of this may come from the social impact on marriage, but part results from the **MARRIAGE (Merging A Right Relationship In A Given Espousal)** itself. In short, their lives are often more fulfilling than singles, but you must do it right.

Fulfillment occurs when the right actions meet a great attitude. Marriage done right gives us a sense of meaning, which the relationship fulfills. VIEW (Vision Including Experienced Wisdom) your marriage as a better alternative in life and enjoy better things than you previously had. Even couples who had to start from scratch can find great reward in knowing their spouse stuck with them through difficulty. Your marriage is a gift we open and enjoy. It's not a burden but a blessing. **FULFILL (Finding Usefulness Leads Faithfully Into Loving Life)** your dreams, create your moments, and make your love story lasting.

Genesis 1:28 God blessed them. God said to them, "Be fruitful, multiply, fill the earth, and subdue it. Have dominion over the fish of the sea, over the birds of the sky, and over every living thing that moves on the earth."

Don't Worry, Be Happy

Sometimes, couples need to hang out together. It is not a date but just a time with each other. Nothing beats just enjoying each other in simple things. Hanging out is free fun and builds camaraderie. It also works as a test of the level of friendship that remains in your relationship. When you're just hanging out with no expectations, conversations run naturally. If problems and judgments are coming up, their frequency tells you how high or low you are on the friendship scale. Those with great conversations and no judgment **SCORE (Sum Counting Our Real Expectations)** high. However, if you can't speak about much without one of you getting an attitude, you have left friendship out of your relationship.

Many grow up thinking that their spouse will be their best friend. It happens sometimes, but we often have friends who **SHARE (Spiritually Hopeful Attitude Repeatedly Encourages)** interests with us that our spouse doesn't have. You can become good friends still. Start by making hang-out time a no-judgment zone. Resist correcting every mistake like a friend does. Find **SIMPLE (Straightforward Information Makes People Learn Easily)** interests you both share and focus your time hanging out there. Enjoying yourself will help filter out bitter speech so you can learn to accept and acknowledge each other respectfully. Start playing around with each other to rebuild camaraderie. Take it slow and grow your friendship when ready.

Proverbs 27:9 Perfume and incense bring joy to the heart;
so does earnest counsel from a man's friend.

You Talk Too Much

People say that knowledge is half the battle. If so, one-sided communication is a source of many problems. One-sided communication occurs when one person dominates the **CONVERSATION (Consideration Of Needs Visibly Exchanged Require Speaking Active Thoughts Into Oral Negotiations)**. At the same time, the other secures their thoughts and does not contribute meaningfully. Typically, this means a power imbalance in your relationship, perhaps from long periods of not respecting your spouse's thoughts, causing them to internalize and shut down. Often, the expressive partners wonder why the passive listener seems to find their conversations boring when others so readily engage them. The other wishes they wouldn't be interrupted while speaking so they would have a voice in the relationship.

The passive partner may never be the most communicative one, but your goal is to ensure you are both heard. Slowing down the conversation to listen will excite your spouse and show them their thoughts are valuable. Practice drawing thoughts out of your spouse. **ASK (Always Seek Knowledge)** them how they are doing and give them time to think out their responses. Try not to interrupt or be insensitive to their point of view. To the passive partner, jot down things you don't want to forget. Find your space to get into the conversation, and try not to change topics rapidly. Show your interest and share the time.

Proverbs 10:19 In the multitude of words there is no lack of disobedience, but he who restrains his lips does wisely.

You Oughta Know

Communication is not just speaking and hearing; it's sharing and understanding. Communication focuses on relaying our thoughts, ideas, intentions, motives, actions, and feelings in a way they are understood and acknowledged beneficially. Our spouses should be the individuals we feel most confident and comfortable communicating with. Couples can get past nearly anything if they **KNOW (Knowledge Needed Or Wisdom)** what's coming and have time to resolve it. We have brainstorming sessions at work where we clear time to resolve problems and find solutions, so why not set times to communicate and work things out the same way in your relationship?

Set aside a time when you agree to place attitudes and work aside so you can **COMMUNICATE (Conversation Of Mature Mutual Understanding Never Is Confusing As Talks End)** competently in your relationship. It's best to focus on the most pressing topic and work out an agreement or resolution rather than get bogged down with unrelated grievances or dumping the past into the present situation. The next day, start with how you are progressing and place a day in between where you are just checking on how each other is doing before moving on to other topics and working on resolving them in succession. Eventually, you will have fewer problems and more time to talk together and make each other the **PRIORITY (Put Responsibilities In Order Requires Immediate Time Yielded)**.

Proverbs 25:12 As an earring of gold, and an ornament of fine gold, so is a wise reprover to an obedient ear

Gotta Get On Movin'

Many of us were not born with a silver spoon in our mouths, but now that you are married, you are the **ADVANTAGE (A Dominate Victory As Needed Talented Assistance Giving Edge)** in life that your spouse needs. Your abilities place your spouse in a position to win at life. Support your spouse's gifts and talents and watch them achieve greatness. Many of us marry people with untapped dreams and potential. It seemed they were going somewhere, but life got in the way. Well, you are their door opener, encouraging and pushing them through. Use it if you are motivated, encouraging, or **SMART (Sharp Minds Are Rapidly Trained)**. The key to the breakthrough or breakout of many successful people is in the supportive hands of a spouse hidden behind the scenes.

Your spouse may be **SMART (Skilled, Musical, Artistic, Resourceful, Talented)** but stalled. Even the most successful of us have dreamed of wanting to do something they put off to achieve other goals. Look for ways to fulfill that dream even if it doesn't look like it initially thought. Achievement brings us the most satisfaction. If they want to play an instrument, it takes time, so encourage them even when they are bad at it. Give suggestions to help them achieve goals in ways they may not have considered. Helping them reach their dreams may open the door to our own, so stay supportive and become the best advantage they could ever have.

2 Timothy 1:6 For this cause, I remind you that you should stir up the gift of God which is in you through the laying on of my hands.

There Goes My Life

Our society places parental advisory labels on movies, video games, music, and anything with content that may negatively impact the development of growing children. In your marriage, you should maintain parentally advised behavior before your kids. Children desire to imitate people they deeply connect with, so watch closely the people and things that influence them. You must ensure you **IMPART (Imitation Means Parentally Advised Restrictions Taken)** the right things. Young children are functional learners who desire to be your carbon copy or **XEROX (Xerography Effectively Reproducing Other Xennials)**. They don't follow speeches; they imitate actions and will obey what you do, not what you say.

Someone said that God doesn't just give us children so we can grow them up. He gives us children so we can finish growing up ourselves. Children have a way of making us look at our lives and take responsibility more seriously than ever. The parentally advised safeguards you place in front of your children should have already been in place in your marriage. Young children learn right from wrong by following what we do. So, how we speak to and about others in front of them matters. We have to avoid arguing in front of them to ensure that the impact of what we **IMPART (Improving My Parental Achievements Requires Tact)** is safe and minimizes things too complex for them to understand emotionally.

Deuteronomy 6:7 and you shall teach them diligently to your children, and shall talk of them when you sit in your house, and when you walk by the way, and when you lie down, and when you rise up.

Fussing and Fighting

Patience is the virtue with which we have a love/hate relationship. We love it most when we mess something up and need time to fix it or make it up to someone. We hate it when we are anxious to receive something we need or desire. Patience isn't just waiting but retaining a good attitude while you endure. Due to a lack of patience, couples unnecessarily fuss when they go somewhere together and rob themselves of a possible good time while traveling and involving themselves in events. *IMPATIENCE (I May Put A Timer If Entering Needless Conflict Endures)* with your spouse will cause mental frustration and often ends in confrontation. Impatience is often about personal image and desire rather than the process of doing what is best for you as a couple.

There is a reason that people who don't feel the need to be on time for everything generally improve their mental health. They take the pressure off. Patience allows you to endure difficult things more straightforwardly. When life is pressing on you, breathe and keep a calm mind. Life is busy, but we should learn to adjust our attitude to avoid making mistakes or making our partner feel rushed. When we stay *CALM (Cool Attitude Lessens Mess)*, we prevent potential problems from erupting. Instead of fussing and fighting, give each other the freedom of fairmindedness, making them more important than any other.

Ecclesiastes 7:8 Better is the end of a thing than its beginning. The patient in spirit is better than the proud in spirit.

Hold On

We all revel in the thrill of victory of the sudden underdog. That person who has fallen at the beginning of a race but gets back up and pushes harder until they overtake the competition and win. Such victory stories give us hope that resilience and perseverance will win out in the end. Some marriages start with such big problems that many don't want to get back up. Know that how you start doesn't have to be how you finish. Our **PROBLEMS (Points Requiring Our Best Listening End Messy Situations)** are opportunities to fix what's wrong in our relationship. Couples who battle early on problems come out into the open and often end up in a more agreeable relationship because they start working out resolutions early, eventually realizing they have addressed the most critical issues, learning to communicate, compromise, and coordinate their efforts.

Starting well is good, but finishing the race is better. Many start fast, but few finish strong. If you are resilient enough, you are strong enough to finish. Fighting doesn't mean you are with the wrong person; it means you are using the wrong relationship skills. The issues you fight over are not as important as how you resolve the conflict. Tackle each problem until there is virtually nothing competing against you. **SHARE (Supporting Healthy Activities Require Effort)** in the fight; you will see enemies fall while you stand again.

2 Timothy 4:7 I have fought the good fight. I have finished the course. I have kept the faith.

Take This Job And Shove It

It is not for everyone, but if you have two incomes, try your best to live off one. Some dual-income families are due to unavoidable circumstances. There is simply a need for the second income to get by, especially in the early years. Other dual-income families are by design. Imagine using one income for all the routine bills and another to handle extra expenses, family plans, and a robust retirement. How you treat your income will determine your outcome. If you use your second **INCOME** *(Inflowing Net Cash Of Money Earned)* for investment, retirement, and emergencies, you may wind up retiring 15 years earlier and much more comfortably. It can be a struggle at times, but if one spouse loses their job, it will have little impact on the household finances.

Some families have discovered that trimming back and having a single-income household works well for them. The working spouse may have to **RETIRE** *(Release Employment To Include Restful Environment)* at a later age. Still, unless the other spouse has a significant income, the money you save on child care expenses, not having an extra car note, which means lower insurance, and home-cooked meals instead of eating out may save the few thousand a month they would have made. Changing our **ROUTINE** *(Route One Usually Takes Is Normal Everyday)* can save the money the other spouse would make and leave both spouses less stressed and more emotionally secure in the long run.

Ecclesiastes 11:2 Give a portion to seven, yes, even to eight;
for you don't know what evil will be on the earth.

Something That We're Not

Some people think being friends with their ex is nice. However, most spouses don't. Many people have a healthy relationship that doesn't work out but ends on good terms, so they maintain a friendly relationship with a former romantic interest. As a single, an ex can be a good friend because they know how to motivate, nurture, and support you. However, we must understand that the friendship must end once we seriously consider getting married because there may be unresolved feelings, attraction, and expectations. You may not want to get back together, but they might, and it may cause *JEALOUS (Jilted Emotions Are Leaving Others Uncomfortably Suspicious)* jitters, making your marriage unstable and unsecured.

Our attachments with an ex who is a friend can emotionally detach us from our spouse during rough seasons by giving us alternative comparisons and internal conflicts that bring up any unresolved feelings beneath the surface. If there is an ex in your life due to children or mutual friends, make sure the line of delineation is apparent. You can remain friendly without being friends. Never have your new love pay for the troubles your ex took you through. They have no say in what goes on in your house and do not have the privilege to voice their opinion about your spouse. Keep the ex out of the next. Be *CLEAR (Communications Leaves Everyone Alertly Responsive)* about your relationship and boundaries that they cannot cross.

John 4:18 for you have had five husbands; and he whom you now have is not your husband. This you have said truly.

My Vote Don't Count

Most couples are partisan pairs, meaning they align politically and belong to the same political party. However, often this is not the case. Many choose their party affiliation based on their upbringing rather than their stance. Political beliefs are not party politics. Our political beliefs range from liberal to conservative, with a significant portion of individuals as political moderates who can agree on some issues with both parties and generally fall into the party, reflecting whether they hold fiscal or social issues as their dominant concerns. That means moderate couples with like political beliefs may support and vote for opposite agendas and opposing candidates. *POLITICS (Policies Of Legislating Is Tactical If Constituents Support)* can be confusing and divisive if respect for each position is absent.

Some couples are from opposing extremes, and it seems their partner should understand, but they don't. Opposing ideologies don't have to become opposition in deeds. Allowing your partner to stick to their convictions without being ridiculed is a sign of growth. If you want to change their opinion, stick to the facts and let them speak for you. Don't let *POLITICS (Plans Of Leaders Instigate Talking In Closed Sessions)* blow up your marriage and make you a different person. Many who fight over politics are fighting over their focus on pet issues and may be close in beliefs. Don't let a position spoil a great marriage. Stay independent and happy.

Titus 3:9 But shun foolish questionings, genealogies, strife, and disputes about the law; for they are unprofitable and vain.

Opinion

Over the past few decades, marriage has become a hot political topic. Debates abound on whether marriage should be regulated by the government or not. We have court cases regarding same-sex marriages and minimum age requirements. There are calls to legalize polygamy and increase proxy weddings for the military. Marriage is still the foundation of a healthy society, increasing the chances that children are well-adjusted and emotionally supported. However, views on the importance and impact have shifted to where we **DISCOVER (Distinguished Instructions Should Create Our Victories Encouraging Reward)** that there is no societal agreement on marriage value and purpose. Given so much controversy, ensuring you are on the same page regarding your marriage and expectations is essential.

Take the marriage poll. Make up a list of questions regarding the purpose of marriage, expectations of husband & wife, financial responsibility, child rearing, in-law relationships, dating and romancing your spouse, sex, and communication. Compare your answers, and you will determine if you and your spouse agree. Discuss the differences, and if they are reasonable, seek to make changes. Ask other couples to take your **POLL (Popular Opinion Learning List)** anonymously to see how your answers compare with other married couples. Then, you will ensure you're walking right and heading in the same direction.

Amos 3:8 Do two walk together, unless they have agreed?

I Wanna Sex You Up

When it comes to the bedroom, men generally are looking for a higher volume of sex, while women desire a higher standard of intimacy. Male sexual connections are visual. The massive amount of testosterone in the male body causes cravings when they see their spouse attractively sexual. Sex is not only hunger but also the way that the male gives love. He feels satisfaction when he sees his partner is equally attracted in response. Males often don't release their emotional **CONNECTION (Cultivating Our Natural Needs Effects Compatibility Through Intimacy Others Negotiate)** until you reciprocate their desire. Rejecting their sexual advance feels like a rejection of the person, leading to dejection, which, when repeatedly endured, increases the possibility he will turn his eyes elsewhere.

Frequency matters as men want more quantity, but women want more quality. Female sexual connections are mental and are prompted by their mind, memories, and emotional motives, meaning they take longer to connect than their male partners. **ROMANCE (Relation Of Mature Attraction Necessitates Captivating Emotions)** is essential because it captures the mind, allowing them to release affection and the attention their counterpart desires. Intimacy is vital to a woman as it allows her to be vulnerable and heals old wounds of the heart. Unlocking her mind and showing that you will protect her is the most attractive a man can be.

Songs of Solomon 4:12 My sister, my bride,
is a locked up garden; a locked up spring, a sealed fountain.

Ball Of Confusion

Communication and integrity are the keys to making your spouse secure. Proper communication is how we receive understanding, causing our minds to be at ease, and personal integrity is how we gain trust, allowing our hearts to be at peace. A spouse who trusts and understands you has no reason to be unsure or afraid. Communication breaks down the walls of **CONFUSION (Communication Often Never Frustrates Until Some Idiot Objects Negotiations)**. You can do everything right, but insecurity and insincerity will arise if you don't communicate well. When a spouse has to guess what has happened or is happening repeatedly, their confidence level will wane. Good communication is not an afterthought that explains away actions but is instead preparation that allows your partner to be part of the process.

When we have lost trust, we often ask our spouse to perform a list of acts to rebuild it. These requirements deal with things ranging from our crowds, choices, curfews, consideration, and getting counseling. However, we primarily need communication with **INTEGRITY (Improving Name Though Ethics Gives Relational Increase Through Yeilding)**. When we talk, communicating with integrity means making the **HARD (Honest, Accountable, Respectful, Dutiful)** choices. Communicating with integrity is the best way to show transparency, allowing your spouse to see things through your eyes and heart to rebuild what was lost.

Proverbs 10:9 He who walks blamelessly walks surely,
but he who perverts his ways will be found out.

Do Something

Thriving marriages are relationships built daily where mutual service is present and agreed upon. Due to both spouses giving 100% mutual service, it is called forgotten intimacy. It becomes so natural we forget it started as a series of choices. When we believe we are with someone who truly is there for us, we become more relaxed and comfortable in our relationships and don't mind serving them in return. Having a **SERVANT (Selfless Employment Requires Vision Advancing Needed Teamwork)** attitude is mutually beneficial. You are more intimate allies so busy acting on behalf of each other that you rarely have unmet needs yourself. We shine brighter as we bring light to our spouses, and they return the light we bring back to our family.

Suppose your spouse is not serving your desires as you want them to. It may be a clue that you are not serving their desires as they want you to. If you desire them to do more, then you should do **MORE (Multiplying Outcomes Require Engagement)**. Step up your game like you still believe you have it. When you see a need or are alerted to your spouse's desire, act on it immediately. Encourage service in your spouse by writing a list of what you appreciate about them. Then speak those things, starting sentences with, "I love it when you…" Recognizing their acts builds their esteem and promotes better responses. Service not only fulfills them, but it also fulfills you.

1 Peter 4:10 As each has received a gift, employ it in serving one another, as good managers of the grace of God in its various forms.

Cut Off Time

Have you noticed how banks, online stores, and logistical companies set cut-off times to place your order so that they can guarantee your delivery? A cut-off time is a set time to complete transactions included in that day's securities, settlements, or delivery schedule. We need to set our own cut-off times to guarantee we can sufficiently manage our own life and marital concerns. Without a cut-off time, our **TRANSACTIONS (Taking Rare Actions Need Some Allotment Coordinating Time Intervening On Negotiating Stoppage)** will overwhelm our evenings. We have marital and personal transactions to close at the end of the day. Some examples are making sure you communicate feelings, dealing with concerns, or getting enough sleep so you will have abundant energy the next day.

Cut-off times keep the system from being overwhelmed. We can get busy working all day and evening, overwhelming ourselves and taking the extra stress out on others. Set a cut-off time. 8 o'clock, 9 o'clock, 10 o'clock, or whatever time you like, but cut off speaking to others on the phone or typing on the computer. Your **CUT-OFF (Coordinate Universal Time Or Force Fight)** time is a limit you set for it to be about you and your spouse. Don't answer the phone unless someone calls back-to-back. If it's not an emergency, get off the phone quickly. It's down time to bring you peace; it's me time to bring relaxation and our time to give intimacy. It's time together.

*Ecclesiastes 3:1 For everything there is a season, and
a time for every purpose under heaven:*

Dream On

Make yourself a bucket list and work on it. A bucket list is a record of achievements and activities we want to do before we kick the proverbial bucket. List all the things that each of you has hoped for and prioritize the ones on both of your lists. Never disparage what your spouse puts on the **BUCKET LIST (Before Usage Canceled, Keep Enjoying Time Living In Style Together)**. If you do, they may remove it because of you, not because they don't want to do it. Some of the things on your spouse's list that you may not want to do now, you may feel differently about experiencing in the future. If they never change, encouraging them to enjoy it with friends is okay. Knocking things off your bucket list helps you stay happy and satisfied.

If you don't like the name bucket list, use some variations such as wish or adventure list. Make a second list to take the guesswork out of anniversaries. Remember the marriage time capsule where you put pictures, letters, and memorabilia inside and pull them out before your anniversary? Add a list of desires so that when you review them each year, you can check if you met them. Your list will give you great ideas on what to do on your upcoming anniversary or birthday. It also allows you to budget ahead of time. You will never have to **GUESS (General Understanding Estimating Simple Stuff)** about what to do again.

*Ecclesiastes 2:10 Whatever my eyes desired, I didn't keep from them.
I didn't withhold my heart from any joy, for my
heart rejoiced because of all my labor,
and this was my portion from all my labor.*

I Want To Know What Love Is

Love is vital in marriage, but many hesitate to accept that others love them just as they are. Being uncomfortable with love isn't as uncommon as many may think. Some may feel unworthy or fear that becoming vulnerable may lead to pain. When you have trouble receiving love or loving yourself, accept that your spouse loves you anyway. Accepting that you are loved is how we learn to love. Those who have trouble receiving love from their parents, friends, or family have problems knowing what **LOVE (Loyal One Values Empathy)** is. You may have to work to convince a spouse that you love them regardless of their hang-ups. You don't have to be perfect to be loved. True love sees value beyond the flaws. Don't be afraid to love somebody or to let somebody love you. We aren't just social beings needing interactions but emotional beings needing love.

Life without love is like lunch without an appetite or a year without spring: everything seems bland. Everyone needs someone to love. It doesn't have to be romantic love. It could be love for a child, a friend, or a pet. But we need to love and be loved. Life with love will have thorns, which means it also has roses. The more we let love fill our hearts and our marriages, the greater satisfaction we may feel. A life without love may not be worthless, but it is **WORTH LESS (Without Occasional Relationships, They Have Less Effective Support Systems)** than a life filled with love.

1 John 4:19 We love him, because he first loved us.

Can't Tell Me Nothing

People who enter relationships at times hold onto destructive attitudes. One such attribute is pride. **PRIDE (Prestige Regarded Is Dignity Enlarged)** is destructive in that it controls input, promotes insecurities, and devastates intimacy. Pride may keep us from accepting our spouse's valid solutions because we were not the source. Prideful actions tell our spouse we are a one-person show where all thoughts, ideas, and suggestions center on us, cutting off the partnership and leaving our spouse isolated. It is crucial to our spouses that they be permitted to help, but **PRIDE (Perhaps Really, I'm Doing Everything)** leaves them out of important events. Growing close to someone whose arrogance pushes you away isn't easy. A sense of entitlement causes indifferent behavior when they can't influence outcomes or control their attitude.

PRIDE (Personal Responsibility In Delivering Excellence) based on self-worth or esteem is positive. Pride based on accomplishments is sketchy because they are rooted in something exterior that we lack control over. People with pride have difficulty accepting they can be wrong, but humility is the most effective antidote to pride. People isolate more often from pride than they do to heal from hurt. While pride argues over who is right, humility does what suits all. Take down pride by learning to be humble and transparent, commit to removing barriers, and trusting your spouse's input. The price of pride is too high; let humility take you lower.

Proverbs 16:18 Pride goes before destruction,
and an arrogant spirit before a fall.

Meet Me Halfway

Working together requires a bit of giving and taking. The workplace has a hierarchy of authority and job descriptions that entail where that authority ends. It's the deal we make when we get hired to work for someone else. We have bosses and workers in the work market to get things done as people **TRADE (Transfer Requiring A Dual Exchange)** their time and talent for an income. However, marriage is not about hiring, hierarchy, or income. It's partnership, sharing, and outcome. Marriage is a relationship of compromise, and you are not your spouse's boss. Compromise is an invitation to collaborate and work out your issues, concerns, and problems. It combines the prefix "Com" with the word "Promise" to relay the thought of making common promises.

The first rule of compromise is that we compromise on preferences, not principles. Our morals and values must remain intact for it to be a partnership. Nevertheless, when the two of you each have a good plan, you can't agree on, you must learn to **COMPROMISE (Concessions Of Marriage Partners Require Orderly Model In Settling Equally)**. Traditional marriages have the husband as the tiebreaker in compromises because it promotes strong men, and he takes the brunt of the consequences of wrong decisions. However, he still needs to listen to the wisdom of his wife. However, you compromise, weigh your options, find the middle ground, and respect each other's opinions. A promise is waiting after you compromise.

Philippians 2:4 each of you not just looking to his own things, but each of you also to the things of others.

Buddy

There is a lot out there telling couples how to have good sex in marriage, but some couples desire to have safe sex. There are various reasons why a couple may want to practice safe sex, such as not being mentally prepared for children, a previous pregnancy that almost killed the mother or the rare occasion that you chose to marry someone with an incurable sexually transmitted **DISEASE (Disorder Includes Symptoms Endemically Affecting Systems Energy)** such as herpes, Hepatitis B, HPV or HIV. If you are afraid, you are not emotionally or financially secure for children, life always seems to provide a way. Yet, these are still decisions you must make. Most objections to safe sex are religious ones based on the belief that if God allows for conception, the child has a purpose for being here. However, religious and non-religious couples must decide what they should do based on their principles.

Marriage limits sexual activity to one partner, so **SAFE (Securing A Friendly Environment)** sex is a choice most don't have to contend with. Even religious objectors use the extraction (pull out) or the rhythm method. They may not be safe sex, but they are safer sex when it comes to unwanted pregnancies. Condoms reduce sensation, but you wear protection to prevent infection. Medications like PrEP are necessary, even with a heterosexual HIV-positive partner. It's your marriage, so what happens in your bedroom is your choice; learn to live with it.

Genesis 38:9 Onan knew that the offspring wouldn't be his; and when he went in to his brother's wife, he spilled his semen on the ground, lest he should give offspring to his brother

Bad Day

No one likes to be wrong, but it is a certainty. We misunderstand and misinterpret things while making assumptions without complete knowledge. It doesn't feel good to be shown you were wrong. Some people double down and dismiss correction, minimizing the issue; others use it as an opportunity to grow. Accepting that we are wrong is the right thing to do. It's how we learn and show our spouses that we are someone they can work with. The moment of embarrassment we face from being wrong is better than the lifetime of regret we could face. When we learn from mistakes, we tend not to repeat them. Trying to be **RIGHT (Reason In Giving Honest Truth)** when everyone else knows you are wrong leads to mistrust, as you show the truth only matters when it's about someone else.

It's okay to be wrong sometimes. What is not acceptable is staying wrong. People persist in wrong only when it doesn't affect them negatively. Others tend to pay the price for their wrong **ACTIONS (Always Complete The Immediate Objective Now Silly)**. If your spouse is paying the price of your unwillingness to admit that you're wrong, it's a stiff price. Correcting mistakes opens up our creativity, ingenuity, and innovation. Admitting your wrong is courage, not weakness, and the path to wisdom. Your spouse needs you to admit quickly and passionately when you're wrong, standing for the truth.

Proverbs 28:13 He who conceals his sins doesn't prosper,
but whoever confesses and renounces them finds mercy.

Rise Up

If you ever had a vision of your future, you would likely see yourself in a good place. You imagined you would be healthy and doing well and saw how your character and how you treat others developed. We all have a picture of the kind of person we would like to be. You know that compassionate, calm, and thoughtful person we admire who is within us longing to get out. However, past problems, hurts, attitudes and feelings keep getting in the way. The picture of the person you could be is there so that you can strive for it. Tackle your issues one at a time. Over **TIME (Taking Intimate Moments Effectively)**, you will see the new you coming out. Suppose you don't know where to start. Begin at the beginning with your childhood disappointments. They dictate a lot of our behaviors. Reevaluating them as moments of shaping can help you rid yourself of any stigmas attached so you can move forward.

A successful marriage comes from a couple growing and reaching their career, community, and character potential. If we strive to improve ourselves daily, we will grow significantly before the year ends. Having a target in mind gives us the strength, motivation, and insight into what we are **BECOMING (Belief Empowering Confidence Offers Motivation In Needed Growth)**. Growth is so contagious that when your spouse sees you reaching your potential, they want to catch up to your success. Daily improvements aren't always easy, but they are always worth it.

Judges 6:12 Yahweh's angel appeared to him, and said to him, "Yahweh is with you, you mighty man of valor!

I Give Myself Away

Do you give to get or give because it's the right thing? Giving can be selfish at its core when we demand a return. There is always an emotional return in giving. Sometimes, it is a sense of achievement and accomplishment. Other times, we give to avoid later regret for passing by someone in need. We give wrong when we expect admiration, position, or compensation, which is more of a **BRIBE (Buying Required Influence Boost Effectiveness)**. Dishonesty is the basis of all bribes, so when people don't understand your motives, you may be bribing instead of giving. You may be able to rent one temporarily, but you can't buy a happy relationship. When we insist on something in return or won't give anymore, our bribery has turned into blackmail, which is no way to give to or treat our spouse.

Winston Churchill said, "We make a living by what we get. We make a life by what we give." Sometimes, the most giving person could be the most self-centered one. Ask yourself why you give. If it's to receive, you may be more selfish than your spouse, who doesn't seem to put as much effort in as you, but what they do is from their heart. Honest giving comes from doing good for others, even when there is no tangible benefit for ourselves. Our emotional **RETURN (Reverse Entry Taken Upon Replacement Need)** should be enough to keep us giving. We don't become poor by giving but become rich, as it liberates our soul. Great givers are great healers, so heal the soul of your relationship by making sure you give for the right reasons.

*Proverbs 21:2 Every way of a man is right in his
own eyes, but Yahweh weighs the hearts.*

Pray

The adage, "The family that prays together stays together," is more than a cliche. Families who consistently devote time to pray regularly increase emotional and sexual fidelity and forgiveness. There are no guarantees, but there are emotional and social benefits when we relay honest feelings and thoughts through prayer. Praying **TOGETHER (Task Of Gathering Everyone Through Healthy, Effective Reasoning)** often informs our thoughts and values of how our spouses feel about what is occurring, leading to better decision-making. Prayer helps cement stronger bonds and affects well-being. Prayer will either consume your wrongdoing or doing wrong will choke the life out of your prayers.

Prayer helps us focus during difficult times. Our goal should be to grow and stay stronger while keeping our connection. However, how you pray makes a difference. It can be damaging when individuals use prayers to promote personal agendas and get their point across about how wrong others are. A commitment to prayer should reflect a **COMMITMENT (Commonly Observed Manners Mean I Think More Effort Needs Taking)** to others. Prayer can help resolve issues when it is not just words but actions. Praying couples look for change in themselves, not their spouse. Prayer is an effort to bring God into your situation. Make sure your marriage is about something more significant. Commit, pray, and stay together.

James 5:16 Confess your offenses to one another, and pray for one another, that you may be healed. The insistent prayer of a righteous person is powerfully effective.

Peacekeeper

What you don't resolve will revolve. Undealt with problems tend to **REPEAT** *(Repetition Echo's Plans Easing Alarmed Thoughts)* themselves returning much worse each time. Making decisions that end the immediate conflict without wiping out the problem is like treating a cold with cough syrup. It handles the symptoms but does not treat the disease. After the issues incubate, they return as much more resilient infections that are difficult to eliminate. Resolving refers to making a firm decision that deals with the issue successfully, and you both will stand by, making that problem obsolete in the future. If you're new to marriage, it may take a lot of trial and error, but as time passes and you understand each other better, you will become better equipped to resolve issues.

Take the time to make good resolutions regarding your disagreements and say bye to that issue forever. Sometimes it is good to slow down and meditate on where you are in your life. Reflection leads to new thoughts and the inner strength of conviction. It causes us to appreciate what we have overlooked and to **RESOLVE** *(Resolution Explaining Situation Offers Leverage Verifying Error)* the things that aren't right. Sometimes, a set plan or formula for who handles what kind of problem can help. Ponder a moment about your life, relationships, and future. You will find great thoughts worth thinking about, which will help your future decision-making and problem-solving.

Matthew 5:9 Blessed are the peacemakers, for
they shall be called children of God.

Ups & Downs

One thing about life that we have to learn to accept is that it fluctuates between good and bad times, highs and lows. Life is about navigating through the ups and downs, and so is marriage. When we are down, we must cultivate an environment that causes us to **GROW (Great Reward Of Working)**. When we are up, it helps to celebrate our gained momentum and reinvigorate our strength. We need a support system to help cultivate or celebrate with us during the highs and lows. Having good friends is great, but as a married couple, you also have a spouse near to help lift you through hard times and celebrate your victories with you. It's essential to have someone in seasons when too many fluctuating times test your resilience and flexibility.

The downs in life teach us how to stay grounded and that we need other people in our lives. Your spouse is the hand that you reach for when life throws dirt on you. They are also there to lift you out of the dirt, give you a hand up, and be someone you can celebrate their high times with without feeling guilty about your lows. They are there to ensure that mistakes become lessons for both to grow. Your **SPOUSE (Spiritual Partner Offering Unique Supportive Environment)** can be a kind word when you're critical, a positive effect during negativity, belief in doubt, and a connection so you never feel alone. Life is understood by looking backward but lived by looking forward. So, walk with your spouse while keeping your hands stable.

Ecclesiastes 4:10 For if they fall, the one will lift up his fellow; but woe to him who is alone when he falls, and doesn't have another to lift him up.

Opposites Attract

Regarding charged particles, opposite forces, such as magnets, attract, and those with identical particles repel. But do opposites attract in relationships? It would be much simpler if we were attracted to people with similar personality traits. Many things seem opposite, such as strengths in our areas of weakness, gifts where we aren't gifted, and people from different upbringings, which are complementary qualities that complete us, not true opposites. Many couples will say that their spouse was just different from others they dated in the past, and that's a good thing. Differences bring appeal when they are on the surface. We enjoy the differences that take us out of our comfort zone so we can **BUILD (Better Utilized Instructions Lifts Doubt)** on the differences.

Differences make our relationships edgy, exciting, and electric. However, if your differences are too significant, they will become problematic. Opposites attract, but core values stick. People who express themselves differently on the outside may have similar principles, stances, and beliefs. We are attracted to outward differences but base intimacy, connectivity, and compatibility on similarities. Internal opposites attract, and then they attack. Couples who vehemently disagree on life will find their relationship essentially **BROKE (Beyond Repair Or Knowingly Eroded)**. A good girl eventually leaves the bad boy to find a good man, and vice versa. Couples should let their differences build them, and their similarities bind them. Building and binding help us become complete as a couple and stay attracted.

Psalm 119:63 I am a companion of all them that fear thee, and of them that keep thy precepts.

Hunger For His Presence

Some say men have four basic appetites: physical, visual, sexual, and emotional. Finding someone today willing and able to cook delicious meals is difficult but appreciated. Using meal prep saves time, but food is not the only way to a man's heart. As we said, men are visual. If you want to be the one woman he looks at, keep yourself up. Things will fade with time, but by then, he's hooked. While your visual appeal is good, you must satisfy his sexual appetite. He will share the work to get what he craves. Finally, men have an emotional *APPETITE (A Pleasing Passion Enjoying Testing Its Temptations Endlessly)* for respect, appreciation, and understanding. Doing these four things will help satisfy your husband.

Women *HUNGER (Having Urges Noticed Grants Effective Relief)* for authentic partnership, protection, passion, and position. Women aren't just looking for a bedtime buddy; they want a true partner in all aspects of life, whether social, relational, business, or emotional. Women look for someone they can build with. 1 in 3 women worldwide has experienced violence and desires a man who protects, not punches. They also require protection from outside stigmas, attacks, and traumas. A man who doesn't protect his woman will find himself alone. Women also want to know that they are meaningful to their spouses. Showing greater passion for her than anyone affirms her position in your heart. Those are her basic needs.

*Proverbs 16:26 The appetite of the laboring man labors for him,
for his mouth urges him on.*

Girl, Don't Let It Get You Down

Don't let your emotions lead; make them serve your commitment and purpose. We never reach the greater good through emotions that cause us to quit. Let your commitment anchor your emotions. Your emotions can go back and forth to each extreme and overwhelm you. Commitment will keep you steady and calm during the storm. The mind knows the value of your relationship and its effect on your life and children. Honoring our good feelings is part of the healing process, leading to a positive, well-adjusted attitude. If we don't **ANCHOR (Attachment Needing Comfort, Humility, Or Respect)** negative feelings in our values, beneficial deeds, and commitment, they will drag us down.

Start by ordering your life by your priorities and not your feelings. Feelings change often, but priorities rarely change. God first, Spouse second, Kids third, work/church fourth, extended family and friends fifth. Give attention to people in the order of your **PRIORITY (Preferred Rank In Our Relationship Is Totally Yours)** list so that no one ever feels neglected or unloved. Next, make sure your character and actions align with your purpose. If you aim to build a well-adjusted family, anger, insults, and frustrations won't accomplish this. Finally, filter everything by the values you are trying to teach and maintain. They will keep you from being cast away and drowning others in emotions trying to drag you down.

Hebrews 6:19 This hope we have as an anchor of the soul, a hope both sure and steadfast and entering into that which is within the veil,

God's Plan

If you want your best life, dream big and work on them. Nothing is wrong with imagining big things, but big dreams don't become reality until you dream and fund them together. Ensure your **PLAN (People Looking Ahead Now)** supports your future. Often, couples have individual retirement plans where the spouse doesn't know the details or have much input on ensuring they have enough for their shared dreams. People who thought they would live only 15 years after they retire outlive their retirement by an additional 10 to 15 years. You don't want to live off your kids because you didn't make proper plans. Many will be left in the cold if government retirement plans like Social Security fail. Prepare to be prepared. Spend time with a financial advisor to see how to get where you need to be

Big dreams happen by working on the more minor things. Discuss your current financial situation long-term goals, and curtail unnecessary spending. Seek a financial planner and make a contingency plan. Your plan is a vehicle that you believe in and act on to reach your goals. Planning helps you fund your **FUTURE (Faithfully Used Time Unfolds Right Expectations)**. It's common to place your finances and home in a revocable trust. Assign yourself as the trustee with a successor trustee. A Trust will prevent disputes and avoid probate and extra expensive taxes when you both pass away. Make your plan, stick to it, and live your big dreams.

Proverbs 21:6 The plans of the diligent surely lead to profit; and everyone who is hasty surely rushes to poverty.

Higher Ground

Arguments often get you nowhere fast. Anger and offense will have us react impulsively with an equivalent retaliation. However, going tit for tat only makes things worse. As rational people, we can control ourselves by responding intelligently rather than reacting instinctively. We can choose animal impulse or human intention. The best practice is to take the high road and not get caught up in distress. The high road/ground reflects our ability to show good morals during highly tense or direct difficult times. The **HIGHER GROUND (Hope Inspires Good Habits Ensuring Reasonable Goals Reached Objectively Using Necessary Development)** keeps you from falling victim to attacks on your performance, personality, or person. It shows your spouse and others self-control by not stooping down to their level.

Taking the higher ground is also convicting. When your spouse loses control and sees how calmly you maintain composure, they wonder why they react so differently while you remain in control. It shows your spouse an example that may lead to a desire to gain the same attitude you have. A proper attitude gives **VICTORY (Vision Intentionally Creates The Overcoming Refreshing You)**. Speak what you want your marriage to be and not what you see. The sheer force of a faith-filled positive attitude can shift anything in your favor. Don't say you're doing your best; be your best and see if life doesn't turn around for you.

James 2:13 For judgment is without mercy to him who has shown no mercy. Mercy triumphs over judgment.

Kiss You Back

As children, if someone said something wrong to us, we may have responded, "Sticks and Stones will break my bones, but names will never hurt me." We use it to defend against verbal bullying and tell others how resilient we are. The truth is that being called names does hurt us. Words mold us and may break our hearts or convince us that we deserve no better. We use words to inspire and transform our lives or to attack and tear down our opponents. Sometimes, we are so careless with our words that we attack our spouses and children without thinking about the lasting effects. We may not care about what a stranger says, but the words of someone you love will **MOLD (Make Our Lives Develop)** who you become.

When you speak to your spouse and family, use the same compassion you use for yourself when you feel vulnerable. Some kids grow up never remembering if a parent ever said they loved them, or they recall negative words spoken when getting up in the morning and before sleep at night. People become the hate you give. How you speak for someone reflects your attitude towards them. To reinforce change, empower your words by speaking on behalf of your spouse as you would yourself. The first step in healing is recognizing there is a wound. It's not too late to build what you once tore down. Speak with **HOPE (Healing Our Painful Experiences)** to build up your spouse and family and see if they don't return the love and goodness to you.

James 1:26 If anyone among you thinks himself to be religious while he doesn't bridle his tongue, but deceives his heart, this man's religion is worthless.

You Will Win

We love to win. It is just in our competitive nature. Yet, it is okay to lose a battle to win the war regarding family. A wise strategy will have you losing a battle to gain something of more excellent value. Winning a battle against your spouse may feel good temporarily, but the expense of your spouse's and home's well-being is too high. You will dishearten those you love if you try to win every skirmish. Unnecessary **BATTLES (Beating A Tough Time Leaves Exhausted Spouse)** wear us down to where we can't remember what we are fighting to maintain. Your spouse is your ally, not your enemy. Allies don't always agree on the best tactics, but they agree that whichever strategy they use, they all have input and take the risks and rewards together.

Losing causes us to find other ways to win. You have to feel stronger for your marriage than the issues before you. Always keep your focus. Remember, the overall goal in a relational **BATTLE (Be All That The Lord Expects)** is to find the real enemy while forming our character and maintaining our relationship. Perceptions and expectations instead of actual wrongs done form the basis of most offenses in marriages where the other party's wants were unmet. If you are correct, then it will prove itself. Saying "I told you so" proves your superiority, not your love. Never kick your spouse when they're down, but show compassion and understanding because they have already learned the lesson.

Judges 20:32 The children of Benjamin said, "They are struck down before us, as at the first." But the children of Israel said, "Let's flee, and draw them away from the city to the highways."

Sober

One of the most challenging things is to be married to someone who falls into addictive behavior. Some of our spouses may have had an addiction in the past, but that is vastly different from dealing with an active **ADDICTION (A Dependent Demeanor Is Causing Thought-Inclined Obsessive Need)**, whether it is to drugs, alcohol, gambling, or sex. Because people with an addiction become physically and emotionally abusive when challenged, it isn't easy to have a thriving relationship. Often, the spouse becomes an enabler, covering up their spouse's work absences and making excuses for their behavior. The temptation to help your spouse to keep their job and have some income brought into the home, with the embarrassment of others knowing there are severe problems in the home, has left many as co-dependents.

It is better to allow your spouse to hit rock bottom quickly, forcing them to deal with their behaviors before letting the addiction become firmly established. Being a **CO-DEPENDENT (Cause Of - Deflection Ends Problems Experienced Neutralizing Drugs Effectively Needing Termination)** hides the problem instead of helping. Their self-martyrdom is often obsessed with covering up their spouse's behavior and excusing themselves. Addiction and obsession are not a good mix. Enablers must learn to detach from their savior attitude with love. Don't worry about bitter words; do what is needed and make your spouse get help. You will **ENABLE (Empower Nurturing Advice Before Life Ends)** your healing, not your spouse.

Ephesians 5:18 Don't be drunken with wine, in which
is dissipation, but be filled with the Spirit,

School Days

Hopefully, you took premarital counseling before you got married, but many couples don't. Marriage and parenting are usually the only things we do without learning about them first. The more you know about something, the better you get at it. There are several topics and skills necessary to have a healthy relationship. *STUDY (Search To Understand Devoting Yourself)* about marriage like your future depended on it because it does. Studying gets your mind straight. Study about conflict resolution, emotional intelligence, love languages, and communication. People who don't like studying still like learning. Easy-to-read books like this one can help. Attend seminars or marriage fellowship groups doing activities together. Not only will it build your relationship, but it will also help you understand the way your spouse thinks and what they go through.

We should study because every marriage is tested from the inside and outside. We must have the relational skills needed to learn, adjust, and compromise with our spouse. We also need to set boundaries, responsibilities, and standards to keep those outside of our household from interfering with what is happening inside. Without preparation, you may not pass the *TEST (Temporary Evaluation Showing Talent)* given to you. An occasional refresher on marriage a few times a year may be enough to reinvigorate your marriage. Study, and you might find yourself approved.

Proverbs 1:5 that the wise man may hear, and increase in learning;
that the man of understanding may attain to sound counsel;

Tyrone

While open communication is good at bringing transparency to relationships, marriages open to sharing partners bring troubles. An open marriage is consensual non-monogamy where a couple agrees that it is okay for their partner to have sexual relationships with others as they please. Faithfulness and **MONOGAMY (Mutual Obligation Nurtures Our Giving Affection Marrying You)** are not valued. Some see open marriage as a more honest relationship. Still, like other relationships, people in open relationships often begin sheltering their spouse from their experiences, keeping an unspoken air of deception present in the relationship. Their spouse is their primary partner, but since we cannot dictate our emotions when we have multiple sexual partners, the primary affection may not remain with their spouse.

Related to open marriages are polygyny, referring to a man with multiple wives, and polyandry, referring to a woman with multiple husbands. As mentioned earlier, anything you would not do on your wedding night does not belong in your marriage. Some people in open marriages think they have found their **SOULMATE (Special One Unleashing Love, Making A Treasured Eternity)** only to look for another one. Gitnux research reveals a 38% increase in divorce rates in open marriages when compared to monogamous couples. There is no way to get around the high percentage of mistrust, jealousy, and partner pull-away. Stay monogamous and stay together.

Genesis 16:4 He went in to Hagar, and she conceived.
When she saw that she had conceived, her
mistress was despised in her eyes.

Let's Stay Together

Have you ever told your spouse, "That's our song?" Well, it should be. Sometimes, it's a song you listened to when dating or something included in the wedding ceremony. People have adapted songs for generations. Some tribes give each child a birth song, speaking of the vigor and character expected when they grow up. If the child misbehaves, they place the child in the middle and sing their song so they understand their expectation. The *SONG (Soul Of Natural Growth)* is the anthem representing your marriage and reminding you who you are together. With all the instrumental versions of songs, you can rewrite the lyrics, adapt them to you personally, and have a song to play when you want to celebrate privately or a little romance. As long as you aren't broadcasting or selling it, you won't break any copyright laws, and it provides an opportunity to support the artist who initially made the song.

A fun project would be adding songs yearly until you have your personal best hits album that you can listen to when you go to that special place for your anniversary. Sing your songs to each other playfully, enjoying their tunes and adding a little dance move here and there. Let the *MUSIC (Melody Unites Souls In Chemistry)* bring you closer and lighten the mood. Make a copy for your children and include a birth song specifically made to encourage each one as a special gift from you. Your anthem represents your legacy of love in song; make it great and inspire your creative side.

*Songs of Solomon 1:1-2 The Song of songs, which
is Solomon's. Let him kiss me with
the kisses of his mouth; for your love is better than wine.*

Joy

No matter how many tips, advice, and plans you receive, they won't make you happy unless you apply them. We don't just want long marriages; we want long, happy, and successful marriages. Some of us deal with significant problems to happiness, yet not all unhappy marriages are abrasive or abusive. A person can be unhappy in a marriage where their partner tries to be loving, communicative, and respectful. Happiness is a pleasant emotion externally triggered based on people and events. Joy is a constantly growing internal peace that brings satisfaction to the soul. Because happiness derives from pleasure and joy from peace, you can have one without the other. Together our happiness and joy create our sense of **WELL-BEING** *(We Enjoy Living Life, Bringing Enthusiasm Into Normal Goings).*

No one gets stuck in permanent unhappiness without being part of the problem. Reevaluate the direction of your thoughts and life to find yourself. Happiness dissipates where there is turmoil in your soul. People can try to make you happy, but unless there is **JOY (Just Open Yourself)** inside, it won't last. The idea that you can't be happy unless someone meets certain conditions is a barrier to true joy. If you want to be *HAPPY (Healthy And Personally Positive You)*, find peace and satisfaction because that is the only way to gain and maintain it. Happiness is a journey; joy is a destination, so find your destination of peace and keep journeying there.

Genesis 4:7 If you do what is right, will you not be accepted? But if you refuse to do what is right, sin is crouching at your door; it desires you,

Blended Family

In today's society, many children live in a home with a stepmother/father. It occurs so often that blended families are becoming the norm. When you marry someone, you join your life with their life, including the children. There are no longer their children but our children. The total responsibility rests on both of your shoulders. It takes time, understanding, and planning to ensure the children feel comfortable and accepted in the ***BLENDED FAMILY (Bringing Life Experiences Naturally Drives Everyone's Development Forming A Motivation In Loving You)***. The biological parent needs to establish rules and order with their children so they won't refuse to listen or pay attention to the authority and instruction of their new parent.

The first ingredient in the blend is you. Think of your new kids as bonus children. You often have to fill a void in their life without giving the impression that you are trying to replace or making them feel that liking you betrays a biological parent. Initially, the ***CHILDREN (Changing How Instructions Lovingly Delivered Really Enhances Nurturing)*** may be against the new family, but with some patience and planning, you can win them over. Some kids are easy to win over; others take time. Focus on being supportive and earning their respect. Find things you like to do with them and teach them how to perform and handle things better than they are doing. The reward may come years later, but will be well worth the life and family you build.

Psalm 127:3 Children are indeed a heritage from the LORD, and the fruit of the womb is His reward.

List of Acronyms

For those who love acronyms, there are well over 400 acronyms listed. You will notice some words repeated but form a different acronym. The words included are:

Abuse	Bill	Circle	Defend
Accept	Blame	Class	Defense
Account	Blended Family	Clear	Deeds
Acknowledge	Books	Code	Deplete
Actions	Boost	Co-Dependent	Desire
Addiction	Borrow	Commit	Details
Adjust	Boundaries	Commitment	Devil
Advantage	Bribe	Communicate	Die
Advice	Bucket List	Compare	Discover
Affection	Budget	Complain	Discuss
Agree	Build	Compliments	Disease
Anchor	Busy	Compromise	Divorce
Anger	Buy	Confidence	Doing
Answer	Calendar	Confusion	Door
Apology	Calm	Connection	Duty
Appearance	Capsule	Control	Each
Appreciate	Card	Couples	Effort
Argue	Careless	Conversation	Enable
Asleep	Card	Cook	Energy
Ask	Care	Corner	Ensure
Attractive	Cars	Counselor	Enthusiasm
Avoid	Cease	Credit	Equal
Baggage	Center	Cuddling	Esteem
Balance	Chain	Cut	Evaluation
Basics	Challenge	Cut Off	Exercise
Battle	Change	Dare	Facts
Battles	Channel	Day	Faith
Becoming	Cheap	Debt	Family
Bedroom	Chemistry	Decide	Fashion

Faults	Haven	Joy	Month
Fear	Hear	Justify	Mood
Feedback	Heard	Kind	More
Fight	Heart	Kit	Motivate
Fill	Hearts	Knack	Much
Fire	Help	Know	Music
Flaws	Hide	Lacks	Naked
Focus	Higher Ground	Last	Name
Forgive	Holiday	Late	Naps
Forward	Home	Learn	Nil
Foul	Honest	Life	Notify
Friend	Honey	Like	Oasis
Friends	Honor	Limit	Old
Fulfill	Hope	List	Open
Future	How	Listen	Optimism
Frustrate	If	Loan	Others
Gained	Ignore	Lose	Our
Gap	Ignoring	Love	Outlaws
Gardener	Image	Love Notes	Outlook
Gift	Immature	Manners	Owe
Give	Impart	Marriage	Own
Goal	Impatience	Mature	Pain
God	Impure	Meal	Pains
Golden Rule	Income	Measure	Part
Grab	Influence	Memories	Pass
Grief	In-laws	Mention	Past
Grow	Insecure	Mentoring	Pastor
Growth	Integrity	Message	Path
Guess	Interest	Mime	Peace
Guide	Invent	Mind Bomb	Peaks
Hand	Invest	Mirror	Peeves
Happy	Irritate	Mistake	Perfect
Hard	Issues	Model	Perform
Harm	Jealous	Mold	Photo
Have	Journey	Monogamy	Plan

Poll	Reward	Split	Type
Positive	Right	Suffer	Unmet
Pray	Ring	Support	Unpack
Prayer	Rhyme	Space	Unprotected
Prejudices	Role	Spend	Up
Prepared	Root	Split	Vacate
Prevent	Rope	Spouse	Value
Pride	Rude	Spy	Venting
Priority	Rules	Stand	Victim
Private	Rush	Steal	Victory
Problem	Sabotages	Steer	View
Problems	Sacrifice	Strength	Vision
Projects	Safe	Step Up	Visit
Prompts	Satisfy	Stress	Voice
Protect	Save	Study	Vows
Push	Savings	Tactics	Wait
Queen	Score	Takers	Wash
Ready	Secret	Talk	Waste
Reboot	Secure	Team	Wedding
Recipe	Self	Test	Wellbeing
Reflects	Servant	Theatre	Win
Regret	Sex	Therapy	Wisdom
Remind	Share	Think	Words
Repay	Shift	Thrive	Work
Repair	Shots	Time	Worry
Repeat	Simple	Tip	Worth Less
Replenish	Simplify	Title	Wrong
Represent	Skill	Together	Wrongs
Reset	Slow	Tools	Xerox
Resist	Smart	Trade	Years
Resolve	Solace	Tradition	Young
Respect	Solve	Transactions	Zero
Result	Song	Treasure	Zone
Retire	Soulmate	Trend	
Return	Source	Triage	

Who Sang That Song In The Title

1. Back To God – Reba McEntire
2. All I Can Do Is Write About It – Lynyrd Skynyrd
3. Love's Holiday – Earth, Wind and Fire
4. Forget Me Nots - Patrice Rushen
5. Good Fight – Unspoken
6. Thank You – Keith Urban
7. Some Beach – Blake Shelton
8. Photograph – Ed Sheeran
9. I Swear – All-4-One
10. Lead Me, Guide Me – Elvis Presley
11. Momma Said Knock You Out – LL Cool J
12. Get The Balance Right – Depeche Mode
13. Family Affair – Mary J. Blige
14. Sanctuary – CeCe Winans
15. Roles Reversed – Mimi Webb
16. The Payback – James Brown
17. Listen To What The Man Said – Paul McCartney
18. Responsibility – Dolly Parton
19. Growing Pains – Alessia Cara
20. For The Love of Money – The O'Jays
21. I Won't Back Down – Tom Petty
22. Faithful – Chris Tomlin
23. Blames On Me – Alexander Stewart
24. I'll Be There – The Jackson 5
25. Respect – Aretha Franklin
26. Don't Let Me Get Me – Pink
27. In My Head – Ariana Grande
28. It's Nice To Have A Friend – Taylor Swift
29. Hear Me – Imagine Dragons

30. Roar – Katy Perry

31. There Is None Like You – Lenny LeBlanc

32. Ceasefire – For King & Country

33. Fast Car – Tracy Chapman

34. All Of Me – John Legend

35. Fresh Start – Joan Jett & The Blackhearts

36. Hey, Good Lookin' – Hank Williams

37. A Safe Place To Land – Sara Bareilles

38. Body Language – Queen

39. The Dream Team Is In The House – LA Dream Team

40. She Works Hard For The Money – Donna Summers

41. Work It Out – Tye Tribbett

42. Ignore Me – Betty Who

43. Role Model – Jahmiel

44. Baggage – Bishop Briggs

45. Before He Cheats – Carrie Underwood

46. Speak To My Heart – Donnie McClurkin

47. Playground – Another Bad Creation

48. Rolling In The Deep – Adele

49. Another Brick In The Wall – Pink Floyd

50. Celebration – Kool & The Gang

51. Notified – Mike & Kelly Bowling

52. We're All In The Same Gang – West Coast Rap Allstars

53. We're Gonna Have A Good Time – Rick Springfield

54. Mind Your Own Business – Hank Williams

55. Indescribable – Chris Tomlin

56. Private Eyes – Hall & Oates

57. Love Notes – Upperoom

58. U Get On My Nerves – Jazmine Sullivan

59. Got My Name Changed Back – Miranda Lambert

60. When Doves Cry – Prince

61. Think – Aretha Franklin

62. The Secret Garden – Barry White, El Debarge, Al B. Sure, James Ingram

63. Baby, What A Big Surprise – Chicago

64. Brother, Can You Spare A Dime – Bing Crosby

65. Sweet Thing – Rufus & Chaka Khan

66. At Your Side – The Corrs

67. 1-800-273-8255 – Logic ft. Alessia Cara & Khalid

68. Give Us Clean Hands – Charlie Hall

69. When I Said I Do – Clint Black

70. Turn Off The Lights – Teddy Pendergrass

71. Pictures Of You – The Cure

72. Kindness – Steven Curtis Chapman

73. Walk By Faith – Jeremy Camp

74. Man In The Mirror – Michael Jackson

75. California Dreamin' – The Mamas & Papas

76. Forever Young – Bob Dylan

77. Night Moves – Bob Seger

78. My Stress – NF

79. Legs – ZZ Top

80. ABC – The Jackson 5

81. The Climb – Miley Cyrus

82. God's Got A Blessing – Norman Hutchins

83. You've Been So Faithful – Eddie James

84. Forgive Them Father – Lauryn Hill

85. I Won't Complain – Paul Jones

86. Don't Be Cruel – Elvis Presley

87. Stand By Me – Ben E. King

88. Like A Prayer – Madonna

89. California King – Rihanna

90. Pleasure, Little Treasure – Depeche Mode

91. Blessing On Blessing – Anthony Brown and Group Therapy

92. Manolo – Trip Lee ft. Lecrae

93. Step Up – Linkin Park

94. My Sacrifice - Creed

95. Lyin' Eyes – The Eagles

96. Hold Onto Me – Lauren Daigle

97. Bridge Over Troubled Waters – Simon & Garfunkel

98. Bills, Bills, Bills – Destiny's Child

99. Just The Way You Are – Bruno Mars

100. Always And Forever - Heatwave

101. Let It Go – James Bay

102. Beautiful – Christina Aguilera

103. Time Capsule – Matthew Sweet

104. Careless Whispers – George Michael

105. Magic's In The Makeup – No Doubt

106. Hero – Mariah Carey

107. Oops, I Did It Again – Brittany Spears

108. Put That Woman First – Jaheim

109. Psalm 23 – Mali Music

110. Push It To The Limit – Corbin Bleu

111. Humble And Kind – Tim McGraw

112. Our House – Madness

113. Happy – Pharrell Williams

114. Beautiful Day – U2

115. What A Surprise – The Pointer Sisters

116. I Was Made To Love Her – Stevie Wonder

117. On The Road Again – Willie Nelson

118. Who Am I – Casting Crowns

119. Waterfalls – TLC

120. Take A Fools Advice – Nat King Cole

121. Where Is The Love – Black Eye Peas

122. The Sweetest Taboo - Sade

123. Better Together – Jack Johnson

124. Time After Time – Cyndi Lauper

125. Being With You – Smokey Robinson

126. We Need To Talk – Waterparks

127. Stay Connected – Jackie McCollough

128. Let's Get Married – Jagged Edge ft. DJ Run

129. We Are The World – USA For Africa

130. Be Still – Kelly Clarkson

131. Endless Love – Lionel Richie and Diana Ross

132. Seventy Times 7 – Brand New

133. Treat Them Like They Want To Be Treated – Father MC

134. I Can See Clearly Now – Johnny Nash

135. Celluloid Heroes – The Kinks

136. There You'll Be – Faith Hill

137. Frustrated – Chris Brown

138. Losing My Religion – R.E.M

139. My Head & My Heart – Ava Max

140. Happy Together – The Turtles

141. Moving Forward – Israel Houghton

142. Every Day – Rascal Flatts

143. New Rules – Dua Lipa

144. Nothing Is Lost – The Weeknd

145. With A Little Help From My Friends – The Beatles

146. The Greatest Love Of All – Whitney Houston

147. Hold My Hand – Hootie & The Blowfish

148. I Can't Get No Satisfaction – The Rolling Stones

149. Late Night Talking – Harry Styles

150. Secrets – OneRepublic

151. See A Victory – Elevation Worship

152. They Reminisce Over You – Pete Rock & CL Smooth

153. Thank You – Walter Hawkins

154. Stressed Out – Twenty One Pilots

155. Love Is A Battlefield – Pat Benatar

156. Last Time That I Checc'd – Zee from Kingdom Music (version)

157. Two Lovers – Mary Wells

158. Unbreak My Heart – Toni Braxton

159. I Belong To You – William McDowell

160. Jesus At The Centre – Eben

161. Satisfaction – John Legend

162. Don't Worry, Be Happy – Bobbly McFerrin

163. You Talk Too Much – Run DMC

164. You Oughta Know – Alanis Morissette

165. Gotta Get On Movin' – Menudo

166. There Goes My Life – Kenny Chesney

167. Fussing & Fighting – Bob Marley and the Wailers

168. Hold On – Shawn Mendes

169. Take This Job And Shove It – Johnny Paycheck

170. Something That We're Not – Demi Lovato

171. My Vote Don't Count – Yellopain

172. Opinion – Nirvana

173. I Wanna Sex You Up – Color Me Badd

174. Ball Of Confusion – The Temptations

175. Do Something – Matthew West

176. Cut Off Time – Omarion ft. Kat DeLuna

177. Dream On – Aerosmith

178. I Want To Know What Love Is – Foreigner

179. Can't Tell Me Nothing – Kanye West

180. Meet Me Halfway – Kenny Loggins

181. Buddy – De La Soul ft. Jungle Brothers & Q-Tip

182. Bad Day – Daniel Powter

183. Rise Up – Andra Day

184. I Give Myself Away – William McDowell

185. Pray – MC Hammer

186. Peacekeeper – Fleetwood Mac

187. Ups & Downs – David and Tamela Mann

188. Opposites Attract – Paula Abdul

189. Hunger For His Presence – Jacquelyn Bellamy Copeland

190. Girl, Don't Let It Get You Down – The O'Jays

191. God's Plan – Drake

192. Higher Ground – Stevie Wonder

193. Kiss Me Back – Digital Underground

194. You Will Win – Jekalyn Carr

195. Sober – Pink

196. School Days – Chuck Berry

197. Tyrone – Erykah Badu

198. Let's Stay Together – Al Green

199. Joy – Vashawn Mitchell

200. Blended Family – Alicia Keys

www.ingramcontent.com/pod-product-compliance
Lightning Source LLC
Chambersburg PA
CBHW070106030426
42335CB00016B/2039